Lecture Notes in Computer Science 14539

Founding Editors

Gerhard Goos
Juris Hartmanis

Editorial Board Members

The series Lecture Notes in Computer Science (LNCS), including its subseries Lecture Notes in Artificial Intelligence (LNAI) and Lecture Notes in Bioinformatics (LNBI), has established itself as a medium for the publication of new developments in computer science and information technology research, teaching, and education.

LNCS enjoys close cooperation with the computer science R & D community, the series counts many renowned academics among its volume editors and paper authors, and collaborates with prestigious societies. Its mission is to serve this international community by providing an invaluable service, mainly focused on the publication of conference and workshop proceedings and postproceedings. LNCS commenced publication in 1973.

Antonio Pepe · Gian Marco Melito · Jan Egger
Editors

Segmentation of the Aorta

Towards the Automatic Segmentation, Modeling, and Meshing of the Aortic Vessel Tree from Multicenter Acquisition

First Challenge, SEG.A. 2023
Held in Conjunction with MICCAI 2023
Vancouver, BC, Canada, October 8, 2023
Proceedings

 Springer

Editors
Antonio Pepe 🆔
Graz University of Technology
Graz, Austria

Gian Marco Melito 🆔
Graz University of Technology
Graz, Austria

Jan Egger 🆔
Essen University Hospital
Essen, Germany

ISSN 0302-9743   ISSN 1611-3349 (electronic)
Lecture Notes in Computer Science
ISBN 978-3-031-53240-5   ISBN 978-3-031-53241-2 (eBook)
https://doi.org/10.1007/978-3-031-53241-2

This Springer imprint is published by the registered company Springer Nature Switzerland AG
The registered company address is: Gewerbestrasse 11, 6330 Cham, Switzerland

Paper in this product is recyclable.

Preface

Different countries can have different protocols for the clinical analysis of aortopathies. Clinical-grade guidelines provide a reference for the management of most conditions, but more advanced tools are necessary to standardize the analysis protocol among different aortopathies. In most cases, the analysis consists of the 2D measurement of the aortic diameters in cross-sectional views that are orthogonal to the aorta. A fully automatic 3D segmentation of the aortic tree can support clinical work from both a quantitative and a visual perspective. Furthermore, a mesh representation of the aortic tree can be combined with computational fluid dynamics simulations to better understand the specific dynamics of blood flow, disease onset, and progression.

The SEG.A. 2023 challenge (https://multicenteraorta.grand-challenge.org/) was organized as a satellite event of the Medical Image Computing and Computer Assisted Interventions 2023 (MICCAI 2023) conference, focusing specifically on robustness, visual quality, and meshing of automatically generated segmentations of aortic vessel trees from CT imaging. The challenge was organized as a "container submission" challenge, where participants had to upload their algorithms to Grand Challenge in the form of Docker containers. Three tasks were created for SEG.A. 2023.

The main task focused on the sensitivity of the segmentation algorithms on strongly augmented CT scans generated from five distinct cases. The submission of algorithms for this task was split into three phases: during the first phase, participants had the chance to submit up to six containers and test them against two hidden cases. During the second phase, participants could submit up to three containers and test them against all five hidden cases. The top three solutions were selected for the third phase, where the same solutions were tested against the augmented data. The goal was to test the submissions also for their sensitivities to input variations. Participation in subtasks 1 and 2 was optional for the challenge participants. In Subtask 1, the participants could generate a surface mesh representation of the aorta from the input CT scan. The mesh was to be used as input to the established framework TetMesh for volumetric mesh generation. The best solution was that with the lowest scaled mean Jacobian in the final volumetric mesh. In Subtask 2, the participants could generate a surface mesh generation of the aorta for visualization purposes. The solutions were ranked by a team of eight clinical specialists from four different countries. The challenge showed how, for both subtasks, the best solution was not the one with the highest quantitative metrics in terms of shape matching (Dice Score, Hausdorff Distance), but more factors came into play.

The conference was held in a hybrid setting on October 8, 2023, and featured 10 presentations, including an invited talk by a field expert from 1000shapes GmbH. The challenge proceedings consist of 11 papers, including one invited paper on aortopathies from clinical experts. The organizing team members also provided a descriptor for the creation of the dataset. The challenge papers were reviewed in a single-blind manner, each receiving three reviews. The reviewers' comments were required to be addressed and incorporated into the camera-ready version of the accepted papers.

We are grateful to the organizing team members, the authors, and the speakers for contributing to the success and advancements in automatic segmentation, meshing, and visualization of the aortic vessel tree.

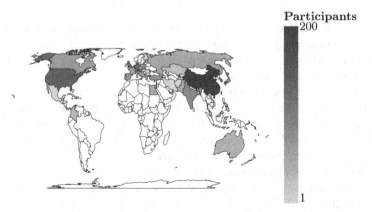

Fig. 1. World map distribution of the participants to the SEG.A. 2023 challenge updated to December 2023. The total number of registered users in the challenge is 508.

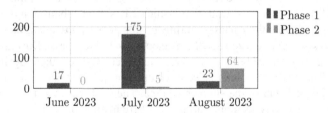

Fig. 2. Number of submissions per month. A total of 215 submissions was recorded in Phase 1, while 69 submissions were documented in Phase 2.

December 2023

Antonio Pepe
Gian Marco Melito
Jan Egger

Organization

Program Committee Chairs

Antonio Pepe	Graz University of Technology, Austria
Gian Marco Melito	Graz University of Technology, Austria
Jan Egger	University Hospital Essen, Germany

Challenge Committee

Alejandro F. Frangi	University of Leeds, UK
Gerhard A. Holzapfel	Graz University of Technology, Austria
Yuan Jin	Graz University of Technology, Austria
Jens Kleesiek	University Medicine Essen, Germany
Jianning Li	University Medicine Essen, Germany
Heinrich Mächler	Medical University of Graz, Austria
Dieter Schmalstieg	Graz University of Technology, Austria
Fen-hua Zhao	Affiliated Dongyang Hospital of Wenzhou Medical University, China

Reviewers

Victor Alves	University of Minho, Portugal
Seyed-Ahmad Ahmadi	NVIDIA, Germany
Fin H. Bahnsen	University Medicine Essen, Germany
Ti-chiun Chang	Merck, USA
Xiaojun Chen	Shanghai Jiao Tong University, China
André Filipe de Sousa Ferreira	University of Minho, Portugal
Luc Duong	École de technologie supérieure, Canada
Shireen Elhabian	University of Utah, USA
Sandy Engelhardt	Heidelberg University Hospital, Germany
Jana Fragemann	University Medicine Essen, Germany
Daniel Haehn	University of Massachusetts Boston, USA
Alexander Hann	University Hospital of Würzburg, Germany
Peter F. Hoyer	University Medicine Essen, Germany
Baoru Huang	Imperial College London, UK
Michael Kamp	University Medicine Essen, Germany

Moon Kim	University Medicine Essen, Germany
Gijs Luijten	University Medicine Essen, Germany
Christian Mayer	Medical University of Graz, Austria
Thomas O'Donnell	Siemens Healthineers, USA
Behrus Puladi	University Hospital RWTH Aachen, Germany
Sascha Ranftl	Graz University of Technology, Austria
Malte Rolf-Pissarczyk	Graz University of Technology, Austria
Peter Roth	University of Veterinary Medicine, Austria
Richard Schussnig	University of Augsburg, Germany
Christina Schwarz-Gsaxner	Graz University of Technology, Austria
Hamidreza Sadeghsalehi	Iran University of Medical Sciences, Iran
Gregor Schiele	University of Duisburg-Essen, Germany
Jan-Niklas Thiel	RWTH Aachen University, Germany
Puxun Tu	Shanghai Jiao Tong University, China
Martin Urschler	Medical University of Graz, Austria

Sponsors

1000shapes GmbH, Berlin (https://1000shapes.com/en/)

AORTIC DISSECTION

MECHANICS - MODELING - SIMULATION

TU Graz LEAD Project on Mechanics, Modeling, and Simulation
of Aortic Dissection (https://biomechaorta.tugraz.at/)

Acknowledgements

The challenge received the support of the *TU Graz LEAD Project on Mechanics, Modeling, and Simulation of Aortic Dissection.* We also want to thank the Computer Algorithms for Medicine Laboratory (https://cafe-lab.org/) members and all the reviewers.

Contents

M3F: Multi-Field-of-View Feature Fusion Network for Aortic Vessel Tree Segmentation in CT Angiography

Yunsu Byeon[1], Hyeseong Kim[1,2], Kyungwon Kim[1], Doohyun Park[1], Euijoon Choi[3], and Dosik Hwang[1,2,4,5(✉)]

[1] School of Electrical and Electronic Engineering, Yonsei University, Seoul, Republic of Korea
dosik.hwang@yonsei.ac.kr
[2] Center for Healthcare Robotics, Korea Institute of Science and Technology, 5, Hwarang-ro 14-gil, Seongbuk-gu, Seoul 02792, Republic of Korea
[3] Department of Artificial Intelligence, Yonsei University, Seoul, Republic of Korea
[4] Department of Oral and Maxillofacial Radiology, Yonsei University College of Dentistry, Seoul, Republic of Korea
[5] Department of Radiology and Center for Clinical Imaging Data Science (CCIDS), Yonsei University College of Medicine, Seoul, Republic of Korea

Abstract. Accurate segmentation of the aortic vessel tree (AVT) in computed tomography angiography (CTA) is crucial for diagnosing and monitoring vascular conditions. However, achieving automated and precise segmentation remains a challenging task due to the intricate structure of the AVT. To address this challenge, we introduce the Multi-Field-of-View Feature Fusion Network (M3F) for the AVT segmentation. M3F processes two distinct 3D patches: a large field-of-view patch for context information and a small field-of-view patch for detailed information. A key aspect of M3F is its fusion mechanism, which integrates the context from the coarse branch with the detail from the fine branch to improve segmentation performance. The M3F (proposed by team name ATB) achieves the 1st place on the second phase of the 2023 MICCAI Seg.A challenge leaderboard. Such remarkable performance highlights M3F's potential for both clinical applications and further research in aortic vessel segmentation.

Keywords: SEG.A. · MICCAI2023 · Medical Image Segmentation · Aortic Vessel Tree Segmentation · Multi-Field-of-View · Feature Fusion

1 Introduction

The aorta, the primary artery in the human body, forms the aortic vessel tree (AVT) in conjunction with its branching arteries. This system is vital for blood circulation throughout the body [4]. Patients with aortic conditions necessitate regular evaluations of these vessels to monitor disease progression [13]. Computed tomography angiography (CTA) has emerged as the leading imaging modality, offering an in-depth view of the AVT [2]. The ideal scenario involves achieving a thorough reconstruction of the AVT and contrasting it with subsequent CTA scans. These comparative assessments identify primary pathology alterations and detect emerging co-morbidities or peripheral shifts. Yet, the manual process is labor-intensive and contouring on a slice-by-slice basis is time-consuming, often becoming impractical in routine clinical settings.

Artificial intelligence (AI)-based automated segmentation techniques [5,12, 15] present a significant potential, especially in their capability for real-time operation and seamless integration into clinical workflows. However, adapting these algorithms to the diverse scanning protocols of various clinical institutions is a challenging problem. Additionally, the limited availability of labeled data due to the cost inefficiency of the annotation process presents another significant concern.

In this work, we introduce a novel AI segmentation algorithm to address these challenges. Firstly, to address the variations in Hounsfield Unit (HU) levels seen in diverse CT images from different institutions, we propose the background HU preprocessing step. Secondly, we propose the Multi-Field-of-View Feature Fusion Network (M3F) based on the Attention U-Net architecture [9]. M3F utilizes a dual-branch structure. Each branch of this structure is trained using a different field-of-view (FOV). During the training phase, we combine the feature maps from both parts, ensuring a comprehensive understanding of the aortic region, from broad patterns to specific details.

The paper is organized as follows. Section 2 details the dataset used in our study, outlines the preprocessing methodologies, and provides an overview of the proposed network architecture. In Sect. 3, we evaluate our model's performance on internal validation set as well as on the second phase test set of the MICCAI 2023 challenge [1]. Finally, the discussion and conclusion are provided in Sect. 4.

2   Materials and Methods

2.1   Dataset Description

In this study, we used AVT (Aortic Vessel Tree) dataset, which is comprised of three institutions, KiTS, Rider, and Dongyang [2,4]. All cases consist of the ascending aorta, aortic arch, brachiocephalic artery, left common carotid artery, left subclavian artery, thoracic aorta, abdominal aorta, and iliac arteries. The dataset also features diverse pathologies, including aortic dissections (AD) and abdominal aortic aneurysms (AAA). An overview of dataset properties, including resolution, the number of axial slices, slice thickness, pathology, and the number of cases, is provided in Table 1. The overall aortic vessel trees are illustrated from different viewpoints in Fig. 1, and the pathological cases of AAA and AD are shown in Fig. 2.

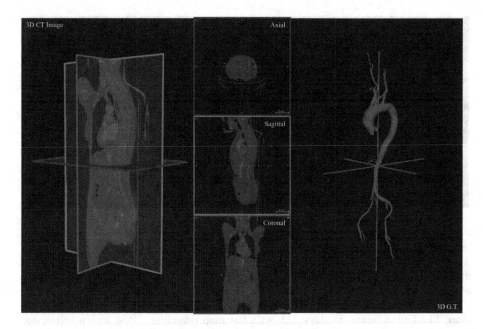

Fig. 1. Example of AVT data.

Table 1. Properties of the aortic vessel trees. Number of axial slices and slice thickness are given as: min/median/max.

Property	KiTS	Rider	Dongyang
Resolution	512 × 512	512 × 512	512 × 666
Axial Slices	94/146/1059	260/1008/1140	122/149/251
Slice Thickness (mm)	0.5/5/5	0.625/0.625/2.5	2/3/3
Pathology	None	AD, AAA	None
Number of Cases	20	18	18

We randomly selected 52 cases for training out of a total of 56 cases from AVT dataset. The remaining 4 cases were used for validation, and no separate testset was used.

2.2 Image Preprocessing

Preprocessing of medical images is important to enhance the robustness and consistency of the medical dataset [11]. In this section, we outline the comprehensive preprocessing workflow, consisting of sequential processing steps to standardize various data properties. The preprocessing workflow involves a series of operations that systematically address heterogeneity. This coherent and strategic approach optimally prepares the dataset for subsequent stages of analysis and model development.

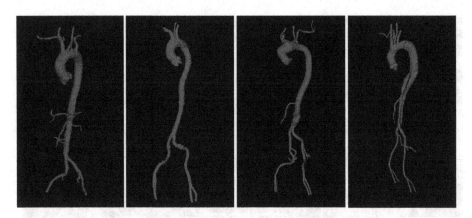

Fig. 2. Aortic vessel trees from a multi-cohort dataset. These images, arranged from left to right, showcase varying z-slice thicknesses: 0.5 mm, 5.0 mm, 0.625 mm (with AAA), and 0.625 mm (with AD). Notably, the image with a z-slice thickness of 5.0 mm displays a reduction in the visibility of thin vessels that are evident in the images with z-slice thicknesses of 0.5 mm or 0.625 mm. Among these, the third image features AAA, characterized by aortic enlargement evident as a localized bulge in the segmentation map. The fourth image displays AD, with the map revealing a false lumen signifying separation within the layers of the aortic wall.

Background HU Preprocessing. The initial step of the preprocessing pipeline is dedicated to addressing variations in background Hounsfield Unit (HU) levels inherent in diverse characteristics in CT images. Through analysis of the HU value histogram, we observed that the HU value ranges varied across the images. To address this inconsistency, the issue was resolved by clipping the values at the leftmost edge, illustrated in Fig. 3. Furthermore, standardization procedures were applied, setting the minimum HU value at −1024. This strategic standardization helps mitigate potential discrepancies originating from distinct medical institutions.

Crop Region of Interest. In accordance with the training cases, an extraction process targeted the non-background region within the CT images. This cropping operation offers two distinct advantages: Firstly, discarding the background region has no impact on the final outcome. Secondly, it significantly reduces image dimensions, thereby greatly improving computational efficiency. We also resampled the image with x, y, z spacing to $0.74 \times 0.74 \times 2.00 \, \text{mm}^3$.

HU Clipping. We observed that the range covering the 0.5 and 99.5 percentiles of aortic vessel tree voxels were limited to the interval [0, 573]. Drawing from this observation, we made an informed decision to establish the HU clipping range as [−100, 600] to also cover the HU values of the neighboring organ region. This selected HU clipping range serves to retain vital details within the aortic vessel tree region while also accommodating a wider spectrum of intensities.

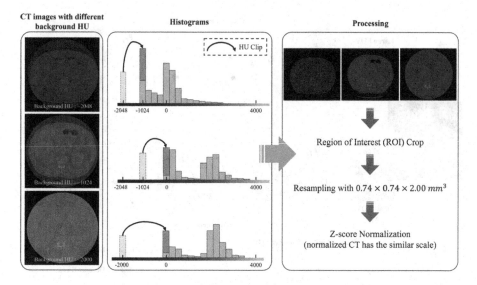

Fig. 3. The overall process of our image preprocessing.

Intensity Normalization. To ensure uniformity and comparability across all images, a z-score normalization was systematically applied to each image in the dataset. This normalization procedure utilizes the mean and standard deviation of each image, effectively aligning the intensity distributions and enhancing compatibility within the dataset.

2.3   M3F: Multi-Field-of-View Feature Fusion Network

The architecture of our method is illustrated in Fig. 4. Inspired by the HookNet [16], designed for segmenting large-scale whole-slide images, we propose the Multi-Field-of-View Feature Fusion Network (M3F). This approach effectively captures multi-field-of-view features, enabling both global context understanding and precise localization.

M3F handles two types of 3D patches: a Large Field-of-View (LFOV) patch with a lower resolution and a Small Field-of-View (SFOV) patch with a higher resolution. The *coarse* branch extracts context from the LFOV patch, while the *fine* branch captures details from the SFOV patch. A key feature of our approach is the fusion of context from the *coarse* branch with the detail from the *fine* branch, targeting enhanced prediction accuracy.

In this section, we describe the three main components of M3F, designed for precise segmentation: (1) the design of the *coarse* and *fine* branches, (2) the input patch sampling strategy, and (3) the Feature Fusion Module (FFM) that combines features from both branches.

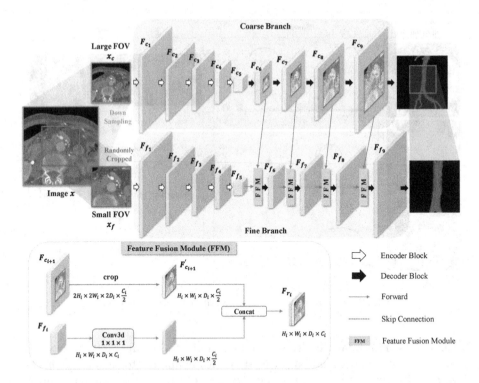

Fig. 4. The overall architecture of M3F. Each branch is designed based on the 3D Attention U-Net framework. For clarity, skip connections and attention gates have been omitted, and the 3D image is depicted as a 2D image.

Coarse and Fine Branches. M3F consists of two primary branches: the *coarse* and *fine* branches. Excluding the FFM, both branches follow the same architectural design and share weights. They are based on the Attention U-Net [9], which integrates attention gates into the conventional UNet [14] structure. During the encoding phase, attention gates allocate weights to features. These weighted features are subsequently merged with decoder features via skip connections, enhancing object localization and segmentation.

Adaptive Patch Sampling. Given a 3D input volume, we extract a sub-volume $x \in \mathbb{R}^{2H \times 2W \times 2D}$ through random cropping. The LFOV image, denoted as $x_c \in \mathbb{R}^{H \times W \times D}$, is obtained by downsampling x uniformly by a factor of 2 across all dimensions. While x_c maintains the same FOV as x, its spatial resolution is halved. The SFOV image $x_f \in \mathbb{R}^{H \times W \times D}$ is derived from x following two guidelines: (1) To avoid spatial misalignment between feature maps of different layer depths in each branch, these maps are constrained to even dimensions. (2) To ensure spatially aligned fusion between the branches, x_f is cropped from x following a $2^P \times 2^P \times 2^P$ grid structure, where P is the number of pooling layer.

Feature Fusion Module. The Feature Fusion Module (FFM) is a core component of the M3F, designed to merge information from the *coarse* branch into the *fine* branch. This merging is accomplished by directly concatenating feature maps from both branches. In the *fine* branch, the decoded feature map F_{f_i} is generated at the ith layer, where i ranges from 6 to 9. Concurrently, the *coarse* branch produces the decoded feature map $F_{c_{i+1}}$ at the $(i+1)$th layer. As F_{f_i} and $F_{c_{i+1}}$ share the same spatial attributes, $F'_{c_{i+1}}$ represents a region within $F_{c_{i+1}}$ that is cropped to spatially align with F_{f_i} for the fusion process. The feature fusion operation can be expressed as:

$$F_{r_i} = Conv_1(F_{f_i}) \oplus F'_{c_{i+1}} \tag{1}$$

where $Conv_1$ denotes $1 \times 1 \times 1$ convolution layer for adjusting the channel size, $\oplus$ denotes the concatenation operation and F_{r_i} denotes the refined feature at the ith layer of *fine* branch.

Through this fusion mechanism, the FFM allows M3F to capture both the broad context from the *coarse* branch and the specific details from the *fine* branch, leading to enhanced segmentation results.

2.4   Network Training

Loss Functions. To address the primary segmentation challenges, we initiate our loss function formulation with a combination of Dice and Focal Loss. Given its capacity to deal effectively with class imbalance in segmentation tasks, Dice Loss L_{Dice} offers a reliable foundation for our composite function. To further alleviate the domination of easy-to-classify pixels and to focus more on the challenging ones, Focal Loss [7], L_{Focal}, is integrated.

While the Dice loss function effectively captures voluminous and thicker vessels, it struggles to capture thin vessels with fewer pixels. To address this limitation and reduce the Hausdorff distance, we use the Hausdorff Distance loss based on distance transforms [6,8]. By leveraging the distance transform map, this loss ensures that the predicted segmentation boundaries closely follow the ground truth. Hausdorff Distance loss is defined as follows:

$$L_{HD}^{DT} = \frac{1}{|\Omega|} \sum_{\Omega} \left[(S_\theta - G)^2 \circ (G_{DTM}^2 + S_{DTM}^2) \right] \tag{2}$$

where G_{DTM} and S_{DTM} denote the distance transform maps of ground truth G and predicted segmentation S_θ, respectively. θ is the parameters of the network and the Ω denotes the grid on which the image I is defined.

For each branch in our M3F architecture, the segmentation loss function is defined as:

$$L_{seg} = \lambda_1 L_{Dice} + \lambda_2 L_{Focal} + \lambda_3 L_{HD}^{DT} \tag{3}$$

where λ_1, λ_2, and λ_3 are the weight parameters. Finally, the total loss function for the M3F model is computed as:

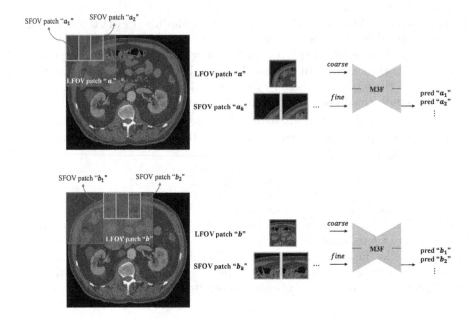

Fig. 5. Visualization of sliding window inference of M3F.

$$L_{total} = L_{seg}^c + L_{seg}^f \tag{4}$$

where L_{seg}^c is the loss function for *coarse* branch and L_{seg}^f is the loss function for *fine* branch. L_{total} ensures that both branches are optimally fine-tuned for precise segmentation.

Data Augmentations. We use intensity augmentations for CTA images, including random gaussian noise, intensity scale, shift, and blurring. We also use spatial augmentation for CTA images, including random rotation and scale in all axes.

2.5   Sliding Window Inference

In the inference stage, we use a sliding window inference strategy, a common approach in patch-wise segmentation (see Fig. 5). For both x_c and x_f, the patches are sampled with an overlap equivalent to half of their patch size. The predictions obtained from the *fine* branch are aggregated to yield the final prediction result. To counteract stitching artifacts and lessen the effects near the window borders, we integrate a Gaussian importance weighting scheme, emphasizing the central voxels during softmax aggregation.

Table 2. The validation set results of aortic vessel segmentation. We computed the mean Dice Similarity Coefficient (mDSC) and 95% Hausdorff Distance (HD95). The best results are **bolded**.

Methods	mDSC ↑	HD95 (mm) ↓
Attention U-Net [9]	0.9295 ± 0.0085	13.7603 ± 10.3299
nnU-Net [3]	0.9373 ± 0.0065	9.2718 ± 5.5383
M3F	**0.9395 ± 0.0078**	**8.1490 ± 7.6858**

Table 3. Overall performance of top-ranking teams on the phase 2 test leaderboard. The best results among 6 teams are **bolded**.

Team	Rank	Mean Position	DSC.50pc ↑ (Position)	DSC.std ↓ (Position)	HD95.50pc ↓ (Position)	HD95.std ↓ (Position)
ATB (ours)	1	**4.5**	0.9173 (9)	0.0204 (5)	**2.6125** (1)	**3.8819** (3)
Brightskies	2	7.5	0.9205 (4)	0.0197 (3)	2.6125 (3)	5.7166 (20)
amrn	3	8	**0.9234** (3)	0.0260 (16)	2.6125 (1)	4.9506 (12)
IWM	4	9	0.9121 (16)	**0.0121** (1)	2.9190 (8)	4.8759 (11)
TeamX	5	11	0.9182 (7)	0.0238 (10)	3.0000 (12)	5.1105 (15)
KARINA	5	11	0.9188 (6)	0.0209 (7)	2.8284 (6)	6.3396 (25)

3 Experiments

3.1 Implementation Details

We use 3D Attention U-net [9] as the backbone network of M3F. We've adjusted the original channel size from 32 to 16 to suit our requirements. The number of pooling layer P is set to 4. The model is trained on a NVIDIA TITAN RTX 24 GB graphics processing unit (GPU) running the PyTorch framework. The AdamW optimizer is used and the initial learning rate is set at 0.001 with a weight decay of 1e−4. We use a batch size of 1 per GPU (with $96 \times 160 \times 160$ patch), and we train the network for 300 epochs (800 iterations per epoch). A Cosine annealing learning rate scheduler is used. The loss weight parameter λ_1 is set to 1, λ_2 is set to 1, and λ_3 is set to 50.

3.2 Results

In this section, we evaluate our model on a single validation set (K1, K6, R1, and R6). We compare the performance of our model with the Attention U-Net and the nnU-Net. The results are shown in Table 2. The proposed method in our validation set achieves 0.940 and 8.149 in terms of mDSC and HD95, respectively, which are approximately 0.0022, 1.1228 better than nnU-Net.

The overall results and ranking from the challenge phase 2 test learderboard are shown in Table 3. Our team achieved the top rank among all competing teams. Specifically, we secured the first position in the 50th percentile of the

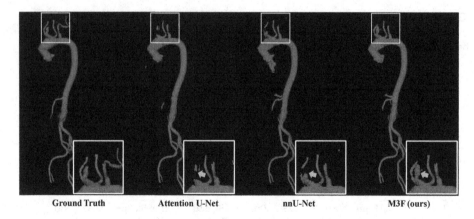

Ground Truth   Attention U-Net   nnU-Net   M3F (ours)

Fig. 6. Visualization of Qualitative Results. We evaluate the qualitative performance of M3F in comparison to other methods.

HD95 metric and ranked third in the standard deviation of HD95. Based on the HD95 metric, our team demonstrated a significant performance difference compared to other leading teams.

The qualitative results are presented in Fig. 6. We have shown one example case from our validation set. We compare the performance of Attention U-Net, nnU-Net, and our methodology. It's evident from the visual comparisons that our model outperforms in detecting thin vascular structures.

4   Discussion

The aim of this research is to develop a method for segmenting the AVT utilizing a deep learning technique. Excluding the main aorta, the AVT comprises vessels as thin as 1mm to 5mm. Considering the resolution of CTA, these thin vessels pose problems as they represent extremely small objects. Excluding the main aorta, the AVT comprises vessels as thin as 1mm to 5mm. Considering the resolution of CTA, these thin vessels pose problems as they represent extremely small objects. To address this, we introduced the Multi-Field-of-View Feature Fusion Network (M3F). M3F was designed to overcome the inherent limitations of convolutional networks that struggle to extract precise features from small objects during the convolution operation. M3F employs a dual-branch encoding strategy, processing both LFOV and SFOV patches. By fusing the feature maps from the coarse and fine branches in LFOV and SFOV, respectively, M3F is trained to consider both the broader context and detailed characteristics. Like this, processing medical images through different encodings is important and effective [10]. Demonstrating its robust performance, our method achieved the top rank in the 2023 MICCAI Seg.A challenge's phase 2, based on evaluations across five unseen cases.

Traditional manual segmentation is both time-consuming and often impractical in clinical settings, emphasizing the pressing need for automated solutions like

AI. Despite the significance of such solutions, MICCAI, which is a leading global conference in medical research, had not previously organized a challenge specifically focused on this area. However, recognizing the growing clinical demand, MICCAI introduced its first challenge on vessel segmentation in 2023.

In this challenge, participants were provided with a dataset of 56 training images. It is worth noting that only vessels larger than 3 mm in diameter were annotated as aortic vessels. These training images came from three different institutions, each having its own specifications like voxel size, slice thickness, reconstruction kernel, and radiation dose. Considering these variations, the challenge not only evaluates the DSC performance but also test the robustness of results against different image variations. Diverse scanning protocols result in variations in HU values within the AVT, making the development of a generalized deep learning model more challenging.

Considering these factors, we designed M3F, which subsequently achieved the top position in phase 2 of the 2023 MICCAI Seg.A challenge. Among the 33 algorithms listed on the leaderboard, our method ranked 1st in HD-50pc, 3rd in HD-std, 9th in DSC-50pc, and 5th in DSC-std, resulting in an overall average rank of 4.5. This performance is notably better when compared to the 2nd placed team, which had an average rank of 7.5. Importantly, this challenge emphasized not only the median value, represented by 50pc, but also the standard deviation (std). Our M3F showed robust performance with its pre-processing steps to normalize institutional characteristics and its model design to consider various ROIs for extraction of vessel feature. The robustness was evident in the std metric, where our method performed well.

Despite the achievements, this study has its limitations. First, our algorithm was evaluated on only five unseen cases, which may not provide sufficient statistical significance. Second, there are instances where our method misses disconnected or thinner vessels, and we have yet to address these issues fully. Third, further analysis on different datasets is required to truly ascertain the effectiveness of our algorithm, especially for thinner vessels. For instance, evaluating our algorithm using vessel segmentation data from retinal images could be beneficial.

In summary, the fact that our methodology ranked first in a global challenge suggests its potential value. In the future, we plan to refine our approach based on more extensive data and a more rigorous evaluation.

Acknowledgements. This research was supported by Basic Science Research Program through the National Research Foundation of Korea funded by the Ministry of Science and ICT (2021R1A4A1031437, 2022R1A2C2008983), Artificial Intelligence Graduate School Program at Yonsei University [No. 2020-0-01361], the KIST Institutional Program (Project No. 2E32271-23-078), and partially supported by the Yonsei Signature Research Cluster Program of 2023 (2023-22-0008).

References

1. Miccai 2023 Seg.A. challenge. https://multicenteraorta.grand-challenge.org/
2. AVT: Multicenter aortic vessel tree CTA dataset collection with ground truth segmentation masks. Data Brief **40**, 107801 (2022)
3. Isensee, F., Jaeger, P.F., Kohl, S.A., Petersen, J., Maier-Hein, K.H.: nnU-Net: a self-configuring method for deep learning-based biomedical image segmentation. Nat. Methods **18**(2), 203–211 (2021)
4. Jin, Y., et al.: AI-based aortic vessel tree segmentation for cardiovascular diseases treatment: status quo (2023)
5. Jun, Y., et al.: Intelligent noninvasive meningioma grading with a fully automatic segmentation using interpretable multiparametric deep learning. Eur. Radiol., 1–10 (2023)
6. Karimi, D., Salcudean, S.E.: Reducing the hausdorff distance in medical image segmentation with convolutional neural networks. IEEE Trans. Med. Imaging **39**(2), 499–513 (2019)
7. Lin, T.Y., Goyal, P., Girshick, R., He, K., Dollár, P.: Focal loss for dense object detection. In: Proceedings of the IEEE International Conference on Computer Vision, pp. 2980–2988 (2017)
8. Ma, J., et al.: How distance transform maps boost segmentation CNNs: an empirical study. In: Medical Imaging with Deep Learning, pp. 479–492. PMLR (2020)
9. Oktay, O., et al.: Attention U-Net: learning where to look for the pancreas. arxiv 2018. arXiv preprint arXiv:1804.03999 (1804)
10. Park, D., et al.: Development and validation of a hybrid deep learning-machine learning approach for severity assessment of covid-19 and other pneumonias. Sci. Rep. **13**(1), 13420 (2023)
11. Park, D., et al.: Importance of CT image normalization in radiomics analysis: prediction of 3-year recurrence-free survival in non-small cell lung cancer. Eur. Radiol. **32**(12), 8716–8725 (2022)
12. Park, Y.W., et al.: Robust performance of deep learning for automatic detection and segmentation of brain metastases using three-dimensional black-blood and three-dimensional gradient echo imaging. Eur. Radiol. **31**, 6686–6695 (2021)
13. Pepe, A., et al.: Detection, segmentation, simulation and visualization of aortic dissections: a review. Med. Image Anal. **65**, 101773 (2020)
14. Ronneberger, O., Fischer, P., Brox, T.: U-Net: convolutional networks for biomedical image segmentation. In: Navab, N., Hornegger, J., Wells, W.M., Frangi, A.F. (eds.) MICCAI 2015. LNCS, vol. 9351, pp. 234–241. Springer, Cham (2015). https://doi.org/10.1007/978-3-319-24574-4_28
15. Shin, H., Kim, H., Kim, S., Jun, Y., Eo, T., Hwang, D.: SDC-UDA: volumetric unsupervised domain adaptation framework for slice-direction continuous cross-modality medical image segmentation. In: Proceedings of the IEEE/CVF Conference on Computer Vision and Pattern Recognition, pp. 7412–7421 (2023)
16. Van Rijthoven, M., Balkenhol, M., Siliņa, K., Van Der Laak, J., Ciompi, F.: HookNet: multi-resolution convolutional neural networks for semantic segmentation in histopathology whole-slide images. Med. Image Anal. **68**, 101890 (2021)

Aorta Segmentation from 3D CT in MICCAI SEG.A. 2023 Challenge

Andriy Myronenko[(✉)], Dong Yang, Yufan He, and Daguang Xu

NVIDIA, Santa Clara, USA
amyronenko@nvidia.com

Abstract. Aorta provides the main blood supply of the body. Screening of aorta with imaging helps for early aortic disease detection and monitoring. In this work, we describe our solution to the Segmentation of the Aorta (SEG.A.23 (https://multicenteraorta.grand-challenge.org/multicenteraorta/)) from 3D CT challenge. We use automated segmentation method Auto3DSeg (https://monai.io/apps/auto3dseg) available in MONAI (https://github.com/Project-MONAI/MONAI). Our solution achieves an average Dice score of 0.920 and 95th percentile of the Hausdorff Distance (HD95) of 6.013, which ranks first and wins the SEG.A. 2023 challenge.

Keywords: Auto3DSeg · MONAI · Segmentation · Aorta

1 Introduction

The aorta serves as the principal artery within the human body. To effectively monitor patients with aortic diseases, it is necessary to regularly examine the vessels for any signs of disease progression [4,6]. Computed tomography angiography (CTA) stands as the conventional imaging technique for clinical evaluation, offering a comprehensive visual of the aortic vessel tree (AVT) [7]. Segmentation of the Aorta (SEG.A.23) 2023 challenge aims to evaluate and compare AI techniques for the best aorta segmentation. The challenge provides the participants with a training set of AVTs and the corresponding manual segmentations from three institutions. The participants are expected to design algorithms for automatic AVT segmentation (see Fig. 1). All the proposed methods are evaluated based on a hidden test set from a fourth institution using Dice Similarity Score (DSC) and 95th percentile of the Hausdorff Distance (HD95). An optional subtasks also asks to create a reconstructed 3D surface geometry, to be evaluated for meshing quality.

2 Methods

We implemented our approach with MONAI [1] using Auto3DSeg open source project. Auto3DSeg is an automated solution for 3D medical image segmentation, utilizing open source components in MONAI, offering both beginner

© The Author(s), under exclusive license to Springer Nature Switzerland AG 2024
A. Pepe et al. (Eds.): SEGA 2023, LNCS 14539, pp. 13–18, 2024.
https://doi.org/10.1007/978-3-031-53241-2_2

and advanced researchers the means to effectively develop and deploy high-performing segmentation algorithms.

The minimal user input to run Auto3DSeg for SEG.A.23 datasets, is

```bash
#!/bin/bash
python -m monai.apps.auto3dseg AutoRunner run \
    --input=./input.yaml --algos=segresnet
```

where a user provided input configuration (input.yaml) including only 3 lines:

```yaml
# This is the YAML file "input.yaml"
modality: CT
datalist: ./dataset.json
dataroot: /data/seg.a23
```

When running this command, Auto3DSeg will analyze the dataset, generate hyperparameter configurations for several supported algorithms, train them, and produce inference and ensemble. The system will automatically scale to all available GPUs and also supports multi-node training. The 3 minimum user options (in input.yaml) are data modality (CT in this case), location of the downloaded SEG.A. dataset (dataroot), and the list of input filenames with an associated fold number (dataset.json). We generate the 5-fold split assignments randomly.

Currently, the default Auto3DSeg setting trains three 3D segmentation algorithms: SegResNet [5], DiNTS [3] and SwinUNETR [2,8] with their unique training recipes. SegResNet and DiNTS are convolutional neural network (CNN) based architectures, whereas SwinUNETR is based on transformers. Here we used only SegResNet.

The simplicity of Auto3DSeg is a very minimal user input, which allows even non-expert users to achieve a great baseline performance. The system will take care of most of the work to anaylyse, configure and optimally utilize the available GPU resources. And for expert users, there are many configurations options that can manually provided to override the automatic values, for better performance tuning.

In the final prediction, we ensemble 15 best model checkpoints of SegResNet (5-folds trained 3 times).

2.1   SegResNet

SegResNet[1] is an encode-decoder based semantic segmentation network based on [5] It is a U-Net based convolutional neural network with deep supervision (see Fig. 2).

The encoder part uses residual network blocks, and includes 5 stages of 1, 2, 2, 4, 4 blocks respectively. It follows a common CNN approach to downsize image dimensions by 2 progressively and simultaneously increase feature size by 2. All convolutions are $3 \times 3 \times 3$ with an initial number of filters equal to 32. The decoder structure is similar to the encoder one, but with a single block per each spatial level. Each decoder level begins with upsizing with transposed

---

[1] https://docs.monai.io/en/stable/networks.html.

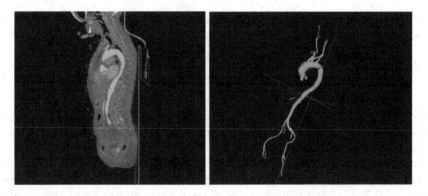

Fig. 1. SEG.A.23 data example of a sagittal 3D CT slice. The provided aorta segmentation (in red) is also shown as a 3D rendering. (Color figure online)

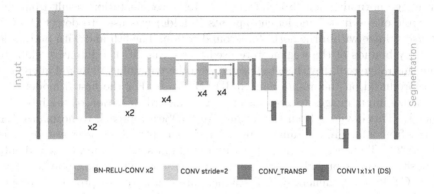

Fig. 2. SegResNet network configuration. The network uses repeated ResNet blocks with batch normalization and deep supervision

convolution: reducing the number of features by a factor of 2 and doubling the spatial dimension, followed by the addition of encoder output of the equivalent spatial level. The number of levels and the region size is automatically configured. We use spatial augmentation including random affine transforming and flipping in all axes, random intensity scaling, shift, noise and blurring.

2.2 Optimization

The models in our solution were trained on an 8-GPU NVIDIA V100 (32 GB) machine. We use the AdamW optimizer with an initial learning rate of $2e^{-4}$ and decrease it to zero at the end of the final epoch using the Cosine annealing scheduler. The batch size is 1 per GPU (effective batch size 8), and weight decay regularization is $1e^{-5}$.

We use the combined Dice + Focal loss. The same loss is summed over all deep-supervision sublevels:

$$Loss = \sum_{i=0}^{4} \frac{1}{2^i} Loss(pred, target^{\downarrow}) \tag{1}$$

where the weight $\frac{1}{2^i}$ is smaller for each sublevel (smaller image size) i. The target labels are downsized (if necessary) to match the corresponding output size using nearest neighbor interpolation.

We trained each of the 5-folds 3 times, and ensemble the final 15 models. Then we used the random cropping of $288 \times 288 \times 288$, and resampled all input images to $0.7 \times 0.7 \times 1.0\,\mathrm{mm}^3$ common resolution. Since one of the goals of SEG.A.23 is to evaluate method robustness to various intensity difference in data from different institutions, we decided to implement an adaptive input 3D CT image normalization. Specifically the Aorta segmentation result from the ensemble of the first 5 model checkpoints (5-folds) was used to detect the CT intensity range within the aorta foreground region. The 5th and 95th percentile intensity bounds of this region were used to re-scale 3D CT intensity globally from this range to 0..1 with soft clipping. And the remaining 10 model inferences were produced on this re-normalized 3D CT image. For the first 5 models, we normalize input images to zero mean, unit standard deviation of the intensity globally. This deviates from the default Auto3DSeg approach to normalize CT images from a foreground range to 0..1. The reasons for this choice was that some SEG.A.23 CT images were in proper Hounsfield units, and some were saved only in positive values probably for compression reasons (which is a non-standard input CT format). Generally, CT scanners are calibrated to produce a proper Hounsfield unit, so in this case our adaptive normalization may not be necessary. This intensity re-normalization approach showed only a slight advantage in our cross-validation experiments, but we decided to keep it.

3   Results

Our inference is an ensemble of 15 SegResNet model checkpoints. Each inference uses a sliding window strategy with an overlap of 0.625. Auto3DSeg uses SlidingWindowInfererAdapt() class from MONAI[2], which automatically manages sliding inference stitching, as well adaptively manages GPU memory (e.g. to offload results fully or partially to RAM). This helps to prevent GPU OOM for large images.

The development environments used for training is presented in Table 1, and was done inside of a docker "nvidia/pytorch:23.06-py3", including PyTorch 2.1 and MONAI 1.2.

Based on our random 5-fold split, the average dice scores per fold are shown in Table 2. An example of the segmentation result of one of the cases from SEG.A.23 dataset is shown in Fig. 3.

---

[2] https://docs.monai.io/en/latest/_modules/monai/inferers/inferer.html

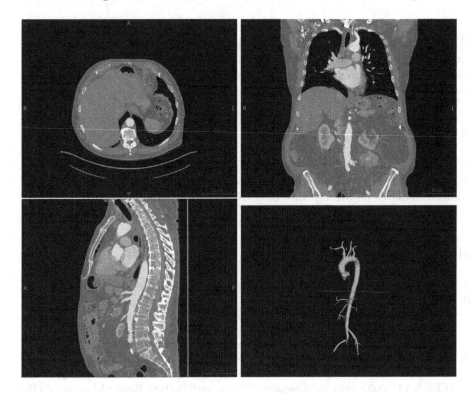

Fig. 3. An example of the segmentation result of one of the cases from SEG.A.23 dataset.

Table 1. Development environments.

Docker	nvcr.io/nvidia/pytorch:23.06-py3
System	Ubuntu 22.04.2 LTS
RAM	400G
GPU (number and type)	8x NVIDIA V100 32G
CUDA version	12.1
Programming language	Python 3.10
Deep learning framework	MONAI 1.2, PyTorch 2.1

Table 2. Average Dice results of a single model based on our 5-fold data split.

Fold 1	Fold 2	Fold 3	Fold 4	Fold 5	Average
0.9298	0.9432	0.9478	0.9401	0.9547	0.94312

On the final hidden challenge dataset, our submission achieved an average Dice score of 0.920 and HD95 of 6.013. SEG.A.23 challenge used a combined metric to rank the methods (accounting for various statistics of Dice and Hausdorff distance) to comprehensively evaluate both method accuracy and robustness. Our submission ranked first on the final test set[3].

4   Conclusion

We described our winning solution to SEG.A. 2023 challenge using Auto3DSeg from MONAI. Our final submission is an ensemble of 15 SegResNet models. Our solution achieves an average dice of 0.920 and HD95 of 6.013, which ranks first on the SEG.A. 2023 final leaderboard.

References

1. Project-MONAI/MONAI. https://doi.org/10.5281/zenodo.5083813
2. Hatamizadeh, A., Nath, V., Tang, Y., Yang, D., Roth, H.R., Xu, D.: Swin UNETR: swin transformers for semantic segmentation of brain tumors in MRI images. In: Crimi, A., Bakas, S. (eds.) International MICCAI Brainlesion Workshop, pp. 272–284. Springer, Cham (2021). https://doi.org/10.1007/978-3-031-08999-2_22
3. He, Y., Yang, D., Roth, H., Zhao, C., Xu, D.: DiNTS: differentiable neural network topology search for 3D medical image segmentation. In: Proceedings of the IEEE/CVF Conference on Computer Vision and Pattern Recognition, pp. 5841–5850 (2021)
4. Jin, Y., et al.: AI-based aortic vessel tree segmentation for cardiovascular diseases treatment: status quo (2023)
5. Myronenko, A.: 3D MRI brain tumor segmentation using autoencoder regularization. In: Crimi, A., Bakas, S., Kuijf, H., Keyvan, F., Reyes, M., van Walsum, T. (eds.) BrainLes 2018. LNCS, vol. 11384, pp. 311–320. Springer, Cham (2019). https://doi.org/10.1007/978-3-030-11726-9_28
6. Pepe, A., et al.: Detection, segmentation, simulation and visualization of aortic dissections: a review. Med. Image Anal. **65**, 101773 (2020). https://doi.org/10.1016/j.media.2020.101773. https://www.sciencedirect.com/science/article/pii/S1361841520301377
7. Radl, L., et al.: AVT: multicenter aortic vessel tree CTA dataset collection with ground truth segmentation masks. Data Brief **40**, 107801 (2022). https://doi.org/10.1016/j.dib.2022.107801. https://www.sciencedirect.com/science/article/pii/S2352340922000130
8. Tang, Y., et al.: Self-supervised pre-training of swin transformers for 3D medical image analysis. In: Proceedings of the IEEE/CVF Conference on Computer Vision and Pattern Recognition, pp. 20730–20740 (2022)

---

[3] https://multicenteraorta.grand-challenge.org/main-task-final-leaderboard/.

A Data-Centric Approach for Segmenting the Aortic Vessel Tree: A Solution to SEG.A. Challenge 2023 Segmentation Task

Ayman El-Ghotni⬤, Mohamed Nabil⬤, Hossam El-Kady⬤,
Ahmed Ayyad$^{(\boxtimes)}$⬤, and Amr Nasr⬤

Brightskies Inc., Alexandria, Egypt
{ayman.elghotni,mohamed.nabil,hossam.elkady,ahmed.ayyad,
amr.nasr}@brightskiesinc.com

Abstract. Data-centric AI is a discipline that focuses on improving the quality and relevance of data used to train AI models. It is a shift from the traditional model-centric approach, which focuses on improving the performance of AI models by tuning the model parameters. This paper presents a data-centric approach for segmenting the aortic vessel tree. The proposed approach consists of a preprocessing pipeline that performs histogram matching and sigmoid windowing, followed by a series of 3D segmentation models. The preprocessing pipeline is designed to improve the contrast and visibility of the vessels in the images, which makes the task easier for the segmentation models. There are three stages of UNet networks each of which performs a different level of segmentation where the result progresses from coarse to fine segmentation. We trained and evaluated the approach to the segmentation of the aorta challenge SEG.A. 2023 dataset. Our approach achieved a Dice Similarity Score of 0.92 ± 0.02 and a Hausdorff Distance (95%) of $6.3\,\text{mm} \pm 5.72$. Our approach produced a segmentation pipeline that accurately captures the complex structure of the aortic vessel tree and is resistant to changes in noise level, contrast, and geometry.

Keywords: Aortic Vessel Tree · Medical Image Segmentation · Data-centric AI · Deep Learning

1 Introduction

The aortic vessel tree (AVT) is a complex network of arteries that supplies blood to the entire body. It is divided into four main parts: the ascending aorta, the aortic arch, the descending aorta, and the abdominal aorta as shown in Fig. 1. Monitoring patients with aortic diseases requires regular screening of the AVT for disease development. The standard image modality for clinical assessment is computed tomography angiography (CTA), which provides a detailed view

A. Pepe et al. (Eds.): SEGA 2023, LNCS 14539, pp. 19–41, 2024.
https://doi.org/10.1007/978-3-031-53241-2_3

of the AVT. However, manual segmentation of the AVT from CTA scans is a time-consuming and labor-intensive task that can take up to a whole day for one scan.

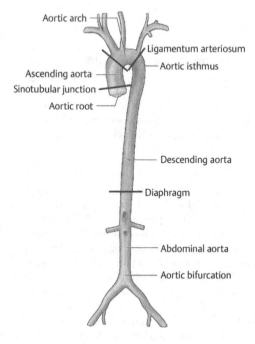

Fig. 1. Anatomy of the aorta [14]. Diagram representing the ascending aorta, aortic arch, descending aorta, abdominal aorta, and the major supra-aortic and abdominal branch vessels.

To address this challenge, AI-supported automatic segmentation methods have been developed. These methods have the potential to run in real time or in the background of the clinical routine, making them more feasible for clinical use. However, there are still challenges to overcome, such as the need to translate these algorithms to work in different clinical institutions and the scarcity of labeled data.

The data from multiple sites with different scanners pose a challenge while training any neural network to effectively segment the AVT. This is because the data distributions vary from site to site, and neural networks are not able to easily generalize to new data distributions. Additionally, the lack of enough labeled data and the complexity of the anatomy of the AVT make it difficult to solve the segmentation problem. In addition to the challenges mentioned above, the inconsistency and variations of manually annotated data from different sites further complicates the segmentation problem, which can impact the accuracy and reliability of the segmentation results and metrics.

Our Major Contributions Are:

1. Introduction of a data-centric approach in order to verify that the scans have consistent spacing, similar appearance, relevant content and consistent value range. Thus making it easier for the neural network to generalize to new distributions easily.
2. Applying model chaining which is technique that uses a pipeline of models to solve a segmentation problem. Each model in the pipeline solves a small part of the problem, and the outputs of the models are combined to produce the final segmentation. This can be more effective than using a single end-to-end model because it allows the models to focus on different aspects of the problem and to learn from each other's mistakes. It significantly reduced overfitting during the training process and increased the overall accuracy.

1.1   Segmentation of the Aorta Challenge 2023

Segmentation of the Aorta (SEG. A. 2023) [4,6,11,15] is a competition organized by Graz University of Technology in Austria and Faculty of Medicine, University of Duisburg-Essen in Germany. The competition was hosted on the grand challenge platform.

The main task of the competition is to develop automatic methods for segmenting the aortic vessel tree (AVT) from computed tomography angiography (CTA) images. This is a challenging task due to the complex and variable appearance of the AVT in CTA images, as well as the limited availability of labeled data. The organizers provided participants with a training set of CTA images and corresponding semi-automated segmentations of AVT from three institutions. The submitted algorithms are ranked using the Dice Similarity Coefficient (DSC), the Hausdorff Distance (HD), and the Sobol's sensitivity indices. The Sobol's indices will quantify the impact of image variations.

The use of a multi-institutional training set is a good way to address the challenge of variability in CTA images. This will help to ensure that the proposed algorithms are robust to different scanning protocols and imaging conditions.

The two optional subtasks of the challenge involve volumetric meshing of the AVT. In the first subtask, a group of clinical specialists will qualitatively evaluate the reconstructed surface geometries. The second subtask quantitatively evaluates the volumetric mesh representation of the AVT using the scaled Jacobian and the number of mesh elements. The goal of both subtasks is to assess the accuracy and robustness of the volumetric meshing algorithms for applications of computational fluid dynamics.

The mission of the challenge is to advance the state-of-the-art in automatic AVT segmentation. The results of the competition will be of benefit to the medical imaging and computational fluid dynamics communities. The competitors will help to develop more accurate and reliable methods for segmenting the AVT, which can be used to improve the diagnosis and treatment of aortic diseases.

1.2   Related Work

Noothout et al. (2018) [10] proposed a method for segmenting the ascending aorta, the aortic arch, and the thoracic descending aorta in low-dose CT scans without contrast enhancement. The method employed a convolutional neural network (CNN) with a receptive field of 131×131 voxels to classify voxels in the axial, coronal, and sagittal image slices. The final segmentation was obtained by averaging the probabilities from the three planes per class, assigning the voxels to the class with highest probability. The study utilized a set of 24 low-dose chest CT scans, randomly selected from a baseline scan collection acquired during the National Lung Screening Trial (NLST). A two-fold cross-validation approach was employed. Ten scans were used for training, ten for testing, and the remaining four scans were used for validation during training. The study emphasized the importance of precise aorta localization due to the homogeneous image intensities resulting from the lack of contrast enhancement. To address varying in-plane resolutions, all scans were resized to an isotropic resolution of 1 mm. The performance of the proposed algorithm was evaluated using the Dice coefficient metric. The results showed Dice coefficients of 0.83 ± 0.07, 0.86 ± 0.06, and 0.88 ± 0.05 for the ascending aorta, the aortic arch, and the descending aorta, respectively.

Fantazzini et al. (2020) [2] proposed a solution for AVT segmentation. The method involved the use of a convolutional neural network (CNN) for the coarse segmentation and localization of the aorta in the CTA volume. Subsequently, three single-view CNNs were employed to segment the aortic lumen, with each view representing the axial, coronal, and sagittal planes. The final segmentation was obtained by concatenating the three views to ensure spatial coherence. The study utilized a dataset provided by IRCCS San Martino University Hospital, which consisted of 80 preoperative CTAs from patients with abdominal aortic aneurysm as the primary pathology. However, patients with other conditions like aortic dissections and thoracic aneurysms were not included in the dataset. The evaluation of the proposed method was conducted using the Dice coefficient (DSC) metric, and the results were reported for each model. The coarse segmentation model achieved a DSC of 0.92 ± 0.01. Furthermore, the axial, coronal, and sagittal views yielded DSC values of 0.92 ± 0.02, 0.92 ± 0.04, and 0.91 ± 0.02, respectively. Finally, the integrated view resulted in a DSC of 0.93 ± 0.02 on a test set comprising 10 CTA scans.

Lyu et al. (2021) [5] proposed a deep learning-based algorithm for segmenting the dissected aorta from CTA images. The algorithm involved two steps. In the first step, a 3D CNN was utilized to divide the 3D volume into two anatomical portions. In the second step, two 2D CNNs based on the Pyramid Scene Parsing Network (PSPnet) were employed to separately segment each specific portion. To enhance the segmentation accuracy, an edge extraction branch based on the Holistically-Nested Edge Detection (HED) network was incorporated into a 2D model. The researchers acquired a dataset consisting of a total of 42 3D volumes, comprising 23,946 slices. For evaluation, the dataset was divided into six groups for a six-fold cross-validation approach. Each group contained seven volumes, with five groups used for training and the remaining group used for testing. The performance of the proposed method was assessed using precision, recall, IOU (Intersection over Union), Dice coefficient, and minDice metrics. The researchers also compared the results of different deep learning-based methods with their proposed method. The Unet3D approach yielded precision, recall, IOU, Dice, and minDice scores of 0.885, 0.863, 0.775, 0.872, and 0.819, respectively. The combination of PSPnet and HED (PSPnet+HED) achieved scores of 0.936, 0.908, 0.852, 0.918, and 0.691 for precision, recall, IOU, Dice, and minDice, respectively. Finally, the proposed method obtained scores of 0.935, 0.914, 0.856, 0.921, and 0.745 for precision, recall, IOU, Dice, and minDice, respectively. Notably, the proposed model demonstrated superior performance in terms of recall, IOU, and Dice metrics, achieving values of 0.914, 0.856, and 0.921, respectively.

Wang et al. (2022) [18] proposed a novel solution for 3D segmentation of the aorta and pulmonary artery, utilizing a two-stage deep learning model. In the first stage, a deep learning model was developed to enhance the contrast of the images. The second stage involved the application of two deep learning models for the segmentation of the aorta and pulmonary artery, using the enhanced images. The dataset for this study was collected from the National Taiwan University Hospital and comprised 179 preoperative chest CT images from patients with lung cancer. The patients were divided into three groups: 59 images were utilized for training the contrast enhancement model, 120 images were used for the segmentation model, and 20 images were used for testing purposes. Evaluation of the segmentation performance was conducted using the Dice Similarity Coefficient as the metric. The achieved results for aortic and pulmonary artery segmentation were reported as 0.97 ± 0.007 and 0.93 ± 0.002 DSC, respectively.

Ömer Faruk Bozkir et al. (2023) proposed a solution that is still under review, in order to segment the thoracic aorta, abdominal aorta, and iliac arteries in both contrast and non-contrast CT images. The dataset utilized for this study was provided by Radl [15] in 2022 and consisted of 38 3D scans obtained from two different institutions. Specifically, the Dongyang institution contributed 18 3D scans with 2,840 axial slices, while the KITS institution provided 20 3D scans with 4,138 axial slices. The approach employed in this study was a data-centric approach, focusing on pre-processing steps. The images were first resized to 256×256 dimensions, followed by normalization. Additionally, Contrast Limited Adaptive Histogram Equalization (CLAHE) was applied to enhance the image quality. Evaluation of the segmentation results utilized sensitivity, specificity, Dice coefficient, and IOU as the metrics. Different models, namely U-Net, U-Net with attention, and Inception U-Netv2, were tested using 2D axial images and a 5-fold cross-validation strategy. The results obtained were as follows: For the U-Net model, the Dice coefficient was 0.895, IoU was 0.81, sensitivity was 0.869, and specificity was 0.99. The U-Net model with attention achieved a Dice coefficient of 0.897, IoU of 0.813, sensitivity of 0.873, and specificity of 0.99. Finally, the Inception U-Netv2 model yielded the best results with a Dice coefficient of 0.904, IoU of 0.827, sensitivity of 0.891, and specificity of 0.99.

2   Methods

This section introduces the AVT segmentation dataset, describes the proposed method, and then provides a comprehensive overview of the preprocessing steps, the models used in each stage, the goal of each model, the post-processing steps and the competition assessment methods.

2.1   Challenge Dataset

Our study used a dataset compilation from 3 centers with varying resolutions, consisting of 56 aortas and their branches. The datasets were obtained through computed tomography angiography (CTA) scans, covering the ascending aorta, aortic arch with head and neck branches, thoracic aorta, abdominal aorta, and iliac arteries leading to the legs [15]. Each scan included a semi-automatically produced segmentation mask of the AVT as ground truth. The segments encompassed the ascending aorta, aortic arch, brachiocephalic, left common carotid, left subclavian artery, thoracic aorta, abdominal aorta, and iliac arteries. However, branches like the celiac trunk or superior mesenteric artery were only visible in cases with more axial slices due to quality variations in the dataset. Our study's segmentation exhibited various pathologies such as aortic dissections (AD) and abdominal aortic aneurysms (AAA).

Initially, we hypothesized that the data came from different scanners, leading to varied sources of error and potentially hindering model training. This hypothesis was supported by the observation of different slice thicknesses in the scans as shown in Fig. 2. Moreover, the average pixel levels differed significantly between scans from the Rider dataset and those from the KiTS and Dongyang datasets as depicted in Fig. 3.

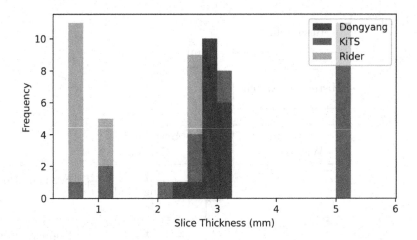

Fig. 2. Distribution of slice thickness for the scans, scans are colored by site

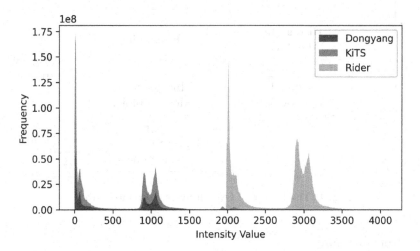

Fig. 3. Pixel level histogram, scans are colored by site, this shows that scans from different sites do not have similar distribution

2.2 System Architecture

The system diagram shown in Fig. 4 illustrates a pipeline of processing steps and neural network models and how they interact with each other. The Base Model, Refining Model and Interpolation Model are all 5-fold UNet networks. Each of the steps and models are further explained in details in the upcoming sections.

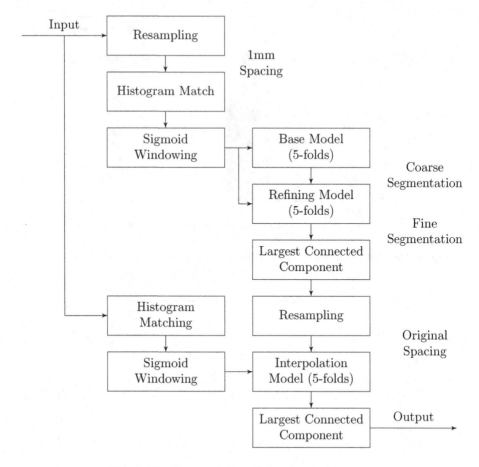

Fig. 4. The Proposed Overall System Architecture.

2.3 Preprocessing

The training data for the model underwent a series of preprocessing operations to prepare it for optimal use. These operations included resampling, histogram matching, sigmoid windowing, weighted random crops, and standardization.

First to achieve consistent spacing within each scan and account for variations in spacing between different sites and scanners, the CTA scans were resampled using linear interpolation to a uniform spacing of 1-mm in each dimension.

Following the resampling, histogram matching and sigmoid windowing techniques were applied. Histogram matching ensured that voxels representing the same anatomical region occupied a consistent range of values across different scans. To perform the matching, a random image (ID "R11" from the Rider dataset) was selected as the pivot image, and all input images were matched to it using 1024 levels and 7 match points.

Sigmoid windowing involved adjusting the voxel ranges of interest within the CTA scans by setting a window width of 800 Hounsfield Units (HU) and a window center of 1200 HU. This step aimed to suppress unnecessary information within the scans. The selection of these values was based on representative samples randomly chosen from the dataset after histogram matching as well as the histogram of the AVT's Hounsfield Units.

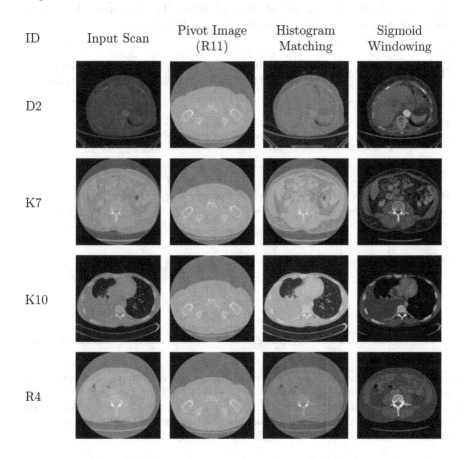

ID	Input Scan	Pivot Image (R11)	Histogram Matching	Sigmoid Windowing
D2				
K7				
K10				
R4				

Fig. 5. The effect of applying histogram matching and sigmoid windowing on input scans from different sites. D2 is a scan from Dongyang dataset, K7 and K10 are scans from KiTS data set and R4 and the pivot image (R11) are scans from Rider dataset.

Figure 5 illustrates the effect of histogram matching and sigmoid windowing on images from different sites, demonstrating the close resemblance in their prospective characteristics after applying both algorithms. Similarly, Fig. 6 presents the results of pixel-level distribution analysis, confirming a closely matched pixel distribution among the images.

To augment the dataset, weighted random crops of the CTA scans were employed. This technique ensured that the input scans provided to the model contained a certain percentage of the AVT, addressing the sparsity of the associated labels. Prior to being inputted into the model, the scans underwent standardization. This process involved scaling the pixel values to achieve a zero mean and unit variance, thereby ensuring a consistent scale and distribution of the input data.

Overall, the preprocessing pipeline aims to enhance the robustness, generalization, and information content of the CTA scans. This, in turn, enables more effective training of models for subsequent analysis or tasks.

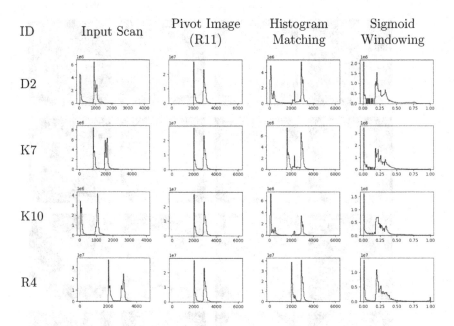

Fig. 6. Pixel level distribution of the scans during different stages of preprocessing. In each of the distribution charts the vertical axis is the frequency and the horizontal axis represents the hounsfield units. D2 is a scan from Dongyang dataset, K7 and K10 are scans from KiTS data set and R4 and the pivot image (R11) are scans from Rider dataset.

2.4   Augmentations

Data enhancement, also known as data augmentation, was leveraged to create additional training data by applying fundamental transformations such as intensity alterations, noise induction, filtering, and rotation [1]. This approach addresses the issue of limited or unbalanced datasets that can lead to overfitting and a degradation in model performance. By expanding and diversifying the training set through data augmentation, the model's ability to generalize and improve predictive accuracy is enhanced.

A series of modifications were constructed using data augmentation techniques to investigate the model's sensitivity to alterations in input data. This allowed us to assess the model's reliability and robustness under varying circumstances, ultimately leading to more accurate and dependable predictions.

To modify the orientation of the scans, a geometric transformation technique known as random rotation was deployed. The rotation was executed parallel to the Z-axis, and the degree of rotation was derived from a normal distribution with a mean of 0° and a standard deviation of 5°. This variation in angle was introduced to mimic possible rotations of the patient. which can occur due to different pathological conditions that affect the patient's stability on the CT table.

To address the motion of the patient during scanning, random shifting was used. The patient's movement was simulated by adding a displacement of up to 2 mm, which is within the typical range of motion observed in patients. A uniform distribution for motion probability was assumed to reflect an equal probability of motion in every direction by the patient.

Furthermore, random contrasts were employed to replicate alterations in intensity. This method was applied to the pixels representing the AVT to mimic the inconsistencies that can occur due to the administration of contrast fluid. The contrast operation could either amplify or reduce the contrast of the AVT within the thorax volume. The contrast value of the CT volume was subjected to a power operation, with gamma as the exponent. Gamma was calculated as shown in Eq. 1.

$$\gamma = e^{\beta} \tag{1}$$

where beta was derived from a normal distribution with a mean of 0 and a standard deviation of 0.05.

Finally, Gaussian noise was added to the images to improve the model's robustness across different image qualities. Gaussian noise with a zero mean and a variable standard deviation was applied. The standard deviation for the Gaussian noise was chosen from a uniform distribution with a lower limit of 0 and an upper limit of 0.03.

2.5   Training

The data was initially divided into 5 folds using the farm hash technique on patient IDs, ensuring reproducibility, prevention of data leakage between experiments, and a near-equal distribution of sites. A UNet3D model [16] with double convolutions, a width of 32, and 8.5 million parameters was employed throughout the three stages. Despite its small size, this model outperformed other deeper models such as UNet3D with ResNet34 and ResNet50 backbones, as well as DeepLabV3+ with the same configurations. An initial learning rate of 0.0005 was utilized, along with a cosine annealing learning rate scheduler in all three stages. The AdamW optimizer with a weight decay of 0.005 was also used in all three stages, with loss functions employed in the three stages consisted of Binary Cross Entropy loss and Dice Loss. The Binary Cross Entropy loss was computed with a pos_weight of 2, assigning a higher weight to positive samples compared to negative samples.

Base Model. In the first model, the objective was to generate a coarse segmentation of the AVT. This was achieved by training the first stage using larger patch sizes of $128 \times 256 \times 256$ with a spacing of 1mm in each dimension.

By training the first model with these settings, a coarse segmentation of the AVT was generated, laying the groundwork for subsequent refinement carried out in the second model.

Connectivity and Edge Refining Model. The purpose of the second model was to improve the output generated by the first model and ensure that the connectivity of the AVT was maintained. It was observed that there were disconnected regions within the AVT in the output of the first model, which needed to be addressed.

To accomplish this, the second model was trained using a smaller patch size of $64 \times 64 \times 64$ and a spacing of 1mm in each dimension. The output of the first model was incorporated into the training process by concatenating it along the channel's axis. Before concatenation, the probabilities from the first model were thresholded to create a binary mask.

In the second model, an additional loss function called topological loss was incorporated to the Binary Cross Entropy and Dice Loss. The chosen topological loss, known as clDice [17] was utilized to ensure the preservation of topology up to homotopy equivalence for binary 3D segmentation. This inclusion of the topological loss effectively guaranteed the connectivity of AVT.

By training the second model with these modifications, the aim was to refine the initial output, address disconnected regions, and improve the overall performance of the AVT model.

Interpolation Refining Model. The third and final model of the training process aimed to refine the interpolation of the output generated by the second model using the nearest neighbor technique. It was observed that there were significant differences in the Dice score when the output of the second model was interpolated to the original spacing of the input scan using linear interpolation versus nearest neighbor interpolation. To ensure a more stable Dice score and smoother edges, a separate model was trained specifically for the refinement of the interpolation process.

The third model was trained using the same patch size as the second model, which was $64 \times 64 \times 64$. The input for training this model was the CT scan after its histogram had been matched to "R11" in its original spacing. The output of the second model, which had been interpolated using nearest neighbor interpolation to match the input scan's original spacing, was concatenated along the channel's axis of the input scan.

By training the third model with these specifications, the aim was to improve the interpolation process, achieve a more stable Dice score, and produce smoother edges in the final output.

2.6   Postprocessing

After the model's segmentation output was used to obtain the binary mask of the AVT, various post-processing techniques were tested to refine the results. It was found that the most effective technique was to select the largest connected component and discard the remaining ones.

This post-processing step was conducted before the third model to ensure that the third model's focus was solely on refining the nearest neighbor interpolation and improving the overall output. Through the selection of the largest connected component, the retention of the main structure of the AVT was aimed for, while smaller, disconnected regions were discarded.

Moreover, to ensure the absence of artifacts resulting from the final segmentation by the third model, the removal of any voxels or structures not connected to the largest connected component was further implemented. This step assisted in enhancing the accuracy and cohesiveness of the final segmentation output.

2.7   Inference

The inference stage leveraged the torchio library [13] for the segmentation of new CTA scans. An inference process involving the usage of overlapping patches with a patch overlap of $16 \times 16 \times 16$ was employed. This strategy aimed to boost the model's confidence in its predictions by facilitating multiple inputs of pixels to the model.

Applying the Hann function to the overlapping areas of patches is crucial for obtaining the final voxel values. This step is instrumental in reducing artifacts and ensuring seamless transitions between adjacent patches in the resulting output. Research studies have consistently demonstrated the effectiveness of the Hann function in artifact reduction and enhancing overall output quality [12]. By minimizing abrupt changes or inconsistencies at patch boundaries, this function facilitates smooth transitions, resulting in a more visually pleasing and coherent final output.

The patch size during inference was kept consistent with that employed during both the training and validation stages. By maintaining such consistency in the patch size, assurance was provided that the model processed the input scans at the same resolution at which it was trained.

2.8   Assessment Methods

The algorithms were assessed using Dice Similarity Coefficient (DSC) [19] and Hausdorff Distance (HD) [3] as evaluation metrics. Furthermore, Sobol' sensitivity indices [7–9] were employed to quantify the influence of various image variations on these evaluation metrics, including intensities, rotations, translations, noise, and blur. The first-order Sobol sensitivity index $S_i^{(1)}$ was used to quantify the impact of each individual input variability on the evaluation metrics (DSC, HD), and the total Sobol sensitivity index $S_i^{(T)}$ was used to measure the interaction between variables in relation to the variation of the evaluation metrics.

To assess the robustness and variability of the algorithm, both DSC and HD were equally influenced by each image variation. The first-order Sobol' indices of each image variation, as shown in Eq. 2, was used to measure this influence.

$$p1 = 1 - \sum_{i=1}^{M} |S_i^{(1)} - \frac{1}{M}| \tag{2}$$

Furthermore, it was ensured that the influence of each image variation does not interact with any other variation. This was measured by calculating the difference between the total-order and first-order Sobol' indices, as shown in Eq. 3.

$$p2 = 1 - \sum_{i=1}^{M} (S_i^{(T)} - S_i^{(1)}) \tag{3}$$

The evaluation metric HD aimed to exhibit a minimal variation with a value as close to 0 as possible. To address the skewed distribution of computed HD values, the evaluation of the HD metric, denoted as p3, incorporates several statistical measures, including the median, variance, and skewness. These rankings were synthesized and their importance emphasized through a weighted aggregation approach. The median-based ranking carried a weight of 0.6, while the weights for variance and skewness are 0.25 and 0.15, respectively, as shown in Eq. 4. This approach ensured a thorough assessment by considering various statistical attributes, enhancing the metric's sensitivity to different data characteristics. Consequently, it enabled a refined perspective on performance beyond a singular measure.

$$p3 = 0.6 * r_{mHD} + 0.25 * r_{\sigma^2 HD} + 0.15 * r_{\mu3,HD} \tag{4}$$

where $\mu3, HD$ is the Fisher's moment coefficient of skewness of the HD distribution.

The evaluation metric DSC aimed to exhibit minimal variation with a value as close to 1 as possible. Similar to the HD metric, the evaluation methodology for DSC follows a comparable approach. It involves assessing the median, variance, and skewness of outcome distributions and ranking them accordingly, as shown in Eq. 5. These rankings were then combined using weights of 0.6, 0.25, and 0.15 to create a balanced final metric, denoted as p4. This final metric encompassed diverse performance aspects and ensured a comprehensive evaluation of the DSC metric.

$$p4 = 0.6 * r_{mDSC} + 0.25 * r_{\sigma^2_{DSC}} + 0.15 * r_{\mu DSC} \tag{5}$$

An intermediate ranking was produced for Eqs. 2, 3, 4, and 5. The final computed ranking was given by the weighted average, as shown in Eq. 6

$$r_{fin} = \frac{(r_1 + r_2)}{6} + \frac{(r_3 + r_4)}{3} \tag{6}$$

3   Results

The results of this paper are presented in this section, first the quantitative analysis of how different preprocessing steps affect the accuracy of the result, then a qualitative analysis of how each neural network stage improves the segmentation task and finally how the proposed system performed during the challenge.

3.1   Quantitative Analysis

To evaluate the effectiveness of histogram matching and sigmoid windowing, two models were trained using identical configurations and hyper-parameters. One model incorporated these pre-processing steps, while the other model did not. The training process took place across two different sites, and subsequently, both models were tested on a third site, which introduced variations in image contrast, noise, rotations, and shifting. The objective was to assess the sensitivity and generalization capabilities of the models.

The findings shown in Fig. 7 revealed that the model trained with histogram matching and sigmoid windowing demonstrated superior generalization. Specifically by having lower standard deviation, higher mode, and higher skewness value closer to 1. These results indicate that the pre-processing steps effectively enhanced the models' ability to adapt to variations in image characteristics and perform reliably across different sites. To test the robustness of the models against Gaussian noise, both models were trained on noisy variations of the test samples as shown in Fig. 8. The model trained with histogram matching and sigmoid windowing was better suited to work on noisy data, as it showed lower error rates than the model trained without these techniques.

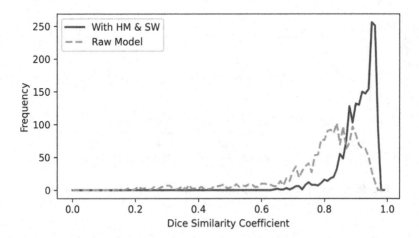

Fig. 7. Distribution of dice similarity coefficient (DSC) when using a model trained with histogram matching and sigmoid windowing (solid line) and another model trained without them (dashed line)

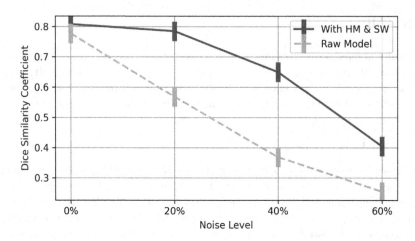

Fig. 8. Anti-noise robustness graph when using a model trained with histogram matching and sigmoid windowing (solid line) and another model trained without them (dashed line)

Figure 9 shows the effect of using a post-interpolation refinement network on the DSC value of the final output. The network improves the DSC by shifting the distribution of DSC values towards 1, indicating a better segmentation.

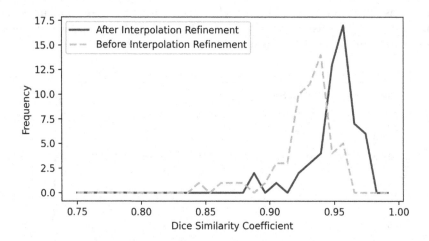

Fig. 9. Effect of using interpolation refinement model on the DSC

3.2   Qualitative Analysis

A comparison of the 3D masks generated by the base model without refinement and those refined afterwards shows that the quality of the masks has improved and the smaller branches that were previously erased are now better defined as shown in Fig. 10. Our previous hypothesis that adding topological loss to the refining model would improve the 3D mask beyond the main branch is supported by this finding. This is because topological loss directly penalizes the smaller branches, which are often incomplete or missing in the base model.

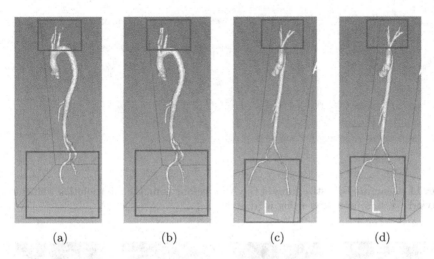

| | | | |
| (a) | (b) | (c) | (d) |

Fig. 10. Generated 3D structures of the AVT after base model only (a, c) and after using refining model (b, d) shown using 3D slicer. Smaller branches highlighted inside the red boxes are better defined after refining model. (Color figure online)

A further quality test was conducted after the interpolation refinement model to assess its usability and importance during segmentation. Figures 11 and 12 show how the surface of the masks becomes smoother and more suitable for surface mesh generation. We found that using nearest neighbor interpolation alone resulted in rough edges on the masks, which the interpolation refinement model addresses.

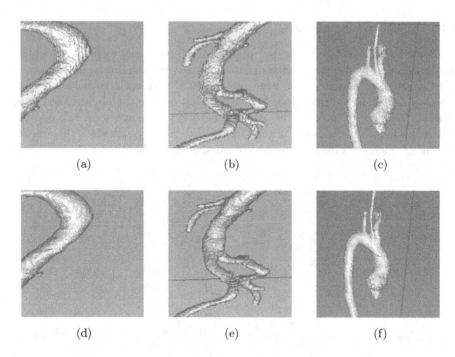

Fig. 11. Generated 3D structures of the AVT before using the interpolation refinement network (a, b, c) and after using it (d, e, f).

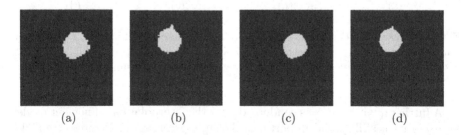

Fig. 12. Sample slices from the segmentation of AVT before using interpolation refinement network (a, b) and after using it (c, d), the borders became much smoother and better defined.

3.3   Challenge Submission

It has been observed that the segmentation of the Aorta challenge has attracted a significant number of participants, with up to 405 participants reported. Among them, 113 valid submissions were made, indicating the wide and significant nature of this challenge.

The segmentation task had 3 different phases, the first of which is for general testing of the container and the initial updates on the algorithms, it had only 2 samples in the hidden test set. The second phase was the cut-off phase, it had 5 samples with more complex structure, the algorithms were ranked based on DSC and HD and the three top performers in second phase will qualify for the final phase. In the final phase the submitted algorithms were tested against 150 augmented test cases and were assessed based on p1, p2, p3 and p4.

Table 1 illustrates how the scores evolved across different phases and methods used during the competition. In the first phase, 6 submissions were made, with only significant submissions mentioned. The phase was kicked off by using the base model as a baseline. It was observed that refining was needed, so a new refining model was added. Then, testing a linear interpolation submission vs the nearest neighbor interpolation submission to return the image in its original spacing was done. It showed that the choice of interpolation technique played a significant role in the accuracy obtained in the evaluation. In phase 2, 2 submissions were made based on the addition of an interpolation model to the algorithm, with the only difference being the training epochs each model underwent where more epochs resulted in a better accuracy. In phase 3, which was the final phase, only 1 submission was allowed, and the same algorithm resulted the best accuracy from phase 2 was submitted.

Table 1. The results of different methods across the 3 phases of the challenge

Phase	Method	DSC			HD		
		mean	50pc	std	mean	50pc	std
1	Base	0.937	0.937	0.012	1.988	1.988	0.558
1	Refine Linear	0.914	0.914	0.012	2.159	2.159	0.257
1	Refine Nearest	0.942	0.942	0.009	2.055	2.055	0.254
2	Interp	0.920	0.912	0.019	7.113	8.483	5.023
2	Interp	0.921	0.920	0.019	6.296	2.612	5.717
3	Interp	0.915	0.918	0.021	7.403	4.491	11.19

The results of the final phase, shown in Figs. 13 and 14, demonstrate the algorithm's robustness and performance. Out of 150 tested variations, only one was not properly segmented, resulting in a DSC of 0.787 and a 95th percentile HD of 132. The average DSC was 0.915 and average 95th percentile HD was 7.4.

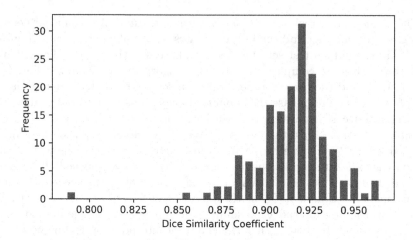

Fig. 13. Distribution of phase 3 Dice Similarity Coefficient

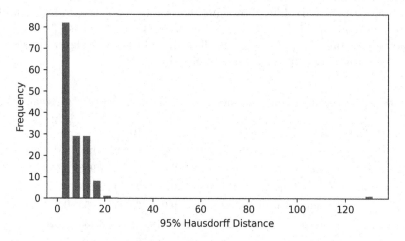

Fig. 14. Distribution of phase 3 95th percentile Hausdorff Distance

3.4 Selected Teams

Table 2 provide summary of the scores of top performing teams in Phase 2. The teams are ranked based on their performance in four categories: HD.50pc, HD.std, DSC.50pc, and DSC.std. Among the teams listed in the table, only the top 3 teams qualified for Phase 3. These teams are ATB, Brightskies, and Amrn.

Table 2. Top Performing Teams in Phase 2

TEAM	Scores			
	HD.50pc	HD.std	DSC.50pc	DSC.std
ATB	**2.6125(1)**	**3.8819(1)**	0.9173(4)	0.0204(3)
Brightskies	2.6125(2)	5.7166(5)	0.9205(2)	0.0197(2)
Amrn	**2.6125(1)**	4.9506(3)	**0.9234(1)**	0.0260(5)
IWM	2.9190(4)	4.8759(2)	0.9121(5)	**0.0121(1)**
TeamX	3.00(5)	5.1105(4)	0.9182(3)	0.0238(4)

4   Conclusion

In this paper, we prove that a data-centric approach combined with a chain of U-Net networks can accurately segment the aortic vessel tree. Several examinations were conducted to assess the importance of histogram matching and sigmoid windowing as preprocessing step, effectively enhancing the models' adaptability to variations in image characteristics and ensuring reliable performance across different sites. The incorporation of these techniques also improved the model's ability to handle noisy data, resulting in lower error rates compared to the model trained without these techniques.

The second stage of the segmentation pipeline utilized topological loss to fix unconnected branches and rectify small edge errors. This led to a significant improvement in the overall accuracy of the output. Additionally, a post-interpolation refinement model was employed to enhance the quality of the masks, resulting in smoother, more accurate, and more realistic segmentations.

Overall, the proposed approach has showed a promise as a method for accurately reconstructing the AVT. It has achieved high accuracy and exhibited strong generalization capabilities across new datasets, enabling its potential application to a variety of patients. This has the potential to enhance the diagnosis and treatment of aortic diseases, including aneurysms and dissections.

In terms of future work, there is room for improvement through hyperparameter tuning and investigate the effect of the randomly chosen pivot on the model performance. By fine-tuning the hyperparameters and carefully monitoring the changes, further enhancements can be made to the approach. Additionally, exploring alternative approaches for monitoring and evaluating changes can provide valuable insights into the performance and robustness of the segmentation model. Expanding the dataset and evaluating the generalization capabilities on larger and more diverse datasets would also contribute to validating the effectiveness of the approach across a wider range of patient populations and imaging conditions.

References

1. Segmentation of the Aorta Challenge: Image variations (2023). https://multicen teraorta.grand-challenge.org/ct-image-variations/
2. Fantazzini, A., et al.: 3d automatic segmentation of aortic computed tomography angiography combining multi-view 2d convolutional neural networks. Cardiovasc. Eng. Technol. **11**(5), 576–586 (2020). https://doi.org/10.1007/s13239-020-00481-z
3. Huttenlocher, D., Klanderman, G., Rucklidge, W.: Comparing images using the Hausdorff distance. IEEE Trans. Pattern Anal. Mach. Intell. **15**(9), 850–863 (1993). https://doi.org/10.1109/34.232073
4. Jin, Y., et al.: AI-based aortic vessel tree segmentation for cardiovascular diseases treatment: status quo. arXiv preprint arXiv:2108.02998 (2021)
5. Lyu, T., et al.: Dissected aorta segmentation using convolutional neural networks. Comput. Methods Programs Biomed. **211**, 106417 (2021). https://doi.org/10.1016/j.cmpb.2021.106417. https://www.sciencedirect.com/science/article/pii/S0169260721004910
6. Maier-Hein, L., et al.: Bias: transparent reporting of biomedical image analysis challenges. Med. Image Anal. **66**, 101796 (2020). https://doi.org/10.1016/j.media.2020.101796. https://www.sciencedirect.com/science/article/pii/S1361841520301602
7. Melito, G.: Sensitivity analysis for model optimization and calibration in type B aortic dissection. Ph.D. thesis, Graz University of Technology (90000), April 2022
8. Melito, G., Jafarinia, A., Hochrainer, T., Ellermann, K.: Sensitivity analysis of a phenomenological thrombosis model and growth rate characterisation. J. Biomed. Eng. Biosci. **7**, 31–40 (2020). https://doi.org/10.11159/jbeb.2020.004
9. Melito, G.M., et al.: Sensitivity analysis study on the effect of the fluid mechanics assumptions for the computation of electrical conductivity of flowing human blood. Reliab. Eng. Syst. Safety **213**, 107663 (2021). https://doi.org/10.1016/j.ress.2021.107663. https://www.sciencedirect.com/science/article/pii/S0951832021002040
10. Noothout, J.M.H., de Vos, B.D., Wolterink, J.M., Isgum, I.: Automatic segmentation of thoracic aorta segments in low-dose chest CT. CoRR abs/1810.05727 (2018). http://arxiv.org/abs/1810.05727
11. Pepe, A., et al.: Detection, segmentation, simulation and visualization of aortic dissections: a review. Med. Image Anal. **65**, 101773 (2020). https://doi.org/10.1016/j.media.2020.101773. https://www.sciencedirect.com/science/article/pii/S1361841520301377
12. Pielawski, N., Wählby, C.: Introducing Hann windows for reducing edge-effects in patch-based image segmentation. PLOS ONE **15**(3), 1–11 (2020). https://doi.org/10.1371/journal.pone.0229839
13. Pérez-García, F., Sparks, R., Ourselin, S.: Torchio: a python library for efficient loading, preprocessing, augmentation and patch-based sampling of medical images in deep learning. Comput. Methods Programs Biomed. **208**, 106236 (2021). https://doi.org/10.1016/j.cmpb.2021.106236. https://www.sciencedirect.com/science/article/pii/S0169260721003102
14. Radiology, G.: Large vessels, July 2019. https://radiologykey.com/large-vessels/
15. Radl, L., et al.: AVT: multicenter aortic vessel tree CTA dataset collection with ground truth segmentation masks. Data Brief **40**, 107801 (2022). https://doi.org/10.1016/j.dib.2022.107801. https://www.sciencedirect.com/science/article/pii/S2352340922000130

16. Ronneberger, O., Fischer, P., Brox, T.: U-Net: convolutional networks for biomedical image segmentation. CoRR abs/1505.04597 (2015). http://arxiv.org/abs/1505.04597

17. Shit, S., et al.: clDice-a novel topology-preserving loss function for tubular structure segmentation. In: Proceedings of the IEEE/CVF Conference on Computer Vision and Pattern Recognition, pp. 16560–16569 (2021)

18. Wang, H.J., et al.: Automated 3d segmentation of the aorta and pulmonary artery on non-contrast-enhanced chest computed tomography images in lung cancer patients. Diagnostics **12**(4) (2022). https://doi.org/10.3390/diagnostics12040967. https://www.mdpi.com/2075-4418/12/4/967

19. Zou, K.H., et al.: Statistical validation of image segmentation quality based on a spatial overlap index. Acad. Radiol. **11**(2), 178–189 (2004)

Automatic Aorta Segmentation with Heavily Augmented, High-Resolution 3-D ResUNet: Contribution to the SEG.A Challenge

Marek Wodzinski[1,2(✉)] and Henning Müller[1,3]

[1] Information Systems Institute, University of Applied Sciences Western Switzerland (HES-SO Valais), Sierre, Switzerland
[2] Department of Measurement and Electronics, AGH University of Krakow, Krakow, Poland
wodzinski@agh.edu.pl
[3] Medical Faculty, University of Geneva, Geneva, Switzerland

Abstract. Automatic aorta segmentation from 3-D medical volumes is an important yet difficult task. Several factors make the problem challenging, e.g. the possibility of aortic dissection or the difficulty with segmenting and annotating the small branches. This work presents a contribution by the MedGIFT team to the *SEG.A* challenge organized during the MICCAI 2023 conference. We propose a fully automated algorithm based on deep encoder-decoder architecture. The main assumption behind our work is that data preprocessing and augmentation are much more important than the deep architecture, especially in low data regimes. Therefore, the solution is based on a variant of traditional convolutional U-Net. The proposed solution achieved a Dice score above 0.9 for all testing cases with the highest stability among all participants. The method scored 1st, 4th, and 3rd in terms of the clinical evaluation, quantitative results, and volumetric meshing quality, respectively. We freely release the source code, pretrained model, and provide access to the algorithm on the Grand-Challenge platform.

Keywords: Aorta · Segmentation · MICCAI · SEGA · Challenge · Deep Learning

1 Introduction

1.1 Overview

The automatic segmentation of the aorta and its branches is one of the most important tasks for cardiovascular system diagnosis and interventions [16]. Aorta diseases like stenosis or dissections pose significant threat to patient's health. Early, automatic detection of such diseases is crucial to ensure timely diagnosis and treatment [15,25]. The problem of aorta segmentation seems to be relatively straightforward for the novel deep learning solutions [13,27] since aorta is clearly visible structure in the magnetic resonance images (MRI), computed tomography angiography (CTA) or sometimes even in computed tomography (CT) without contrast agents. Nevertheless, several challenges make the segmentation task demanding: (i) the possibility of aortic dissections, stenosis, and other morphological changes that increase the data heterogeneity, (ii) the importance of small branches, (iii) the difficulty in acquiring high-quality annotations, (iv) differences in equipment and acquisition protocols between medical centers. These problems, among others, motivated researchers to organize the SEG.A Challenge during MICCAI 2023 conference [1]. This work presents the contribution of the MedGIFT team to the challenge.

1.2   Related Work

The manual aorta segmentation is a time-consuming task prone to human errors. Annotating even a single high-resolution case takes several hours [7], thus it is crucial to speed-up the process by automatic or semi-automatic algorithms. There are only a few studies focused on the fully automatic segmentation of aorta and the whole vessel tree [5,21]. The methods for the automatic aorta segmentation can be divided into different types: (i) deformable models, (ii) tracking models, (iii) deep learning-based models, (iv) others [11]. In this work we focus only on the learning-based methods, for a detailed description of other techniques we refer to the most recent survey [11]. Majority of the existing contributions use some variant of the UNet architecture [2,3,5–7,10,12,14,20,24, 26,30,32]. Almost all of the works use the deep network directly on input volume, after downsampling that makes it possible to train the architecture with GPU acceleration. In contrast, the work by Fantazzini *et al.* [6] employs a combined 2-D/3-D approach where the 3-D network performs the initial aorta segmentation and then the 2-D networks fine-tune the segmentation mask to capture fine-details. The reported Dice coefficient (DSC) varies from 0.82 [14] to even 0.97 [5], however they cannot be directly compared because different datasets, splits, and even modalities are used. The reported dataset size varies from just several cases [14] to more than thousand [7]. The reported processing time also varies strongly from a fraction of second [2] or even several minutes [7,30] per case. Since the currently available contributions cannot be directly compared, the SEG.A challenge is strongly motivated and may provide a large-scale benchmark of the current-state-of-the-art. In this work, we combine the strongest aspects of the already existing contributions and propose high-quality, stable algorithm for the automatic segmentation of the aortic vessel tree.

1.3   Design Choices

Several factors motivated our design choices:

1. The ground-truth annotation of the aortic vessel tree is time-consuming. The provided training set for the method development consists of only 56 cases. Therefore, the proposed solution should operate in an extremely low data regime.

2. One of the most important factors is the algorithm stability and robustness. Therefore, it is crucial to ensure that the solution works correctly even in the most difficult scenarios.
3. The training set consists of CTA scans from various centers with different intensity distributions, thus, requiring a careful approach to the intensity normalization and training augmentation.
4. The small aorta branches are hardly visible and substantial downsampling may reduce their segmentation quality.

These factors motivated us to propose a traditional 3-D CNN based on the UNet architecture, instead of using more novel architectures based on e.g. Vision Transformers [22]. We argue that with such a low amount of training data the network architecture is significantly less important than the data preparation, preprocessing, and augmentation. Moreover, it may even turn out that inductive bias introduced by CNNs is beneficial. Therefore, we decided to:

1. Use 3-D residual UNet with proven usefulness in numerous tasks.
2. Apply heavy data augmentation consisting of several randomly permuted transformations providing substantial variability to the training set.
3. Use relatively large volume shape: $400 \times 400 \times 400$ requiring significant computational resources and training time.

1.4 Contribution

In this work, we present our contribution to the SEG.A challenge organized during the MICCAI 2023 conference. We propose and evaluate 3-D CNN architecture based on residual UNet and show the importance of data preprocessing and augmentation. The proposed contribution is among the best-performing ones and arguably the most stable one in terms of the Dice coefficient. We freely release the source code, pretrained model, and provide access to the algorithm on the Grand-Challenge platform.

2 Method

2.1 Preprocessing

The input volumes are resampled to $400 \times 400 \times 400$, clipped to the $[-700, 2300]$ range, and then normalized to the $[0-1]$ range before any further operations.

2.2 Augmentation

During training, the data is augmented by: (i) random affine transformation, (ii) random intensity transformation, (iii) random Gaussian noise, (iv) random flipping (all axes), (v) random motion artifacts, (vi) random anisotropy transformation, (vii) random Gaussian blurring. The transformations are applied in random order, each with a probability equal to 0.5. The augmentation is implemented using

TorchIO library [17]. Moreover, before training the data was offline augmented by elastic transformations to generate 15000 augmented cases. The reason for performing the elastic augmentation before training was related to the computational complexity of this transformation and the resulting CPU bottleneck.

2.3   Deep Network

A dedicated neural network based on the 3-D ResUNet architecture was implemented. The network takes as input BxlxHxWxD volumes and outputs segmentations with the same shape. The details related to the network architecture are available in the associated repository [29].

2.4   Objective Function and Training

The objective function is a linear combination of two loss terms: (i) Soft Dice Loss, and (ii) Focal Loss, with the same weight for both the loss terms [4].

Fully supervised approach was employed for the network training. The AdamW was used as the optimizer, with an exponentially decaying learning rate scheduler. The network was trained until convergence on the validation set. Additional experiments with 5-fold cross-validation were performed. No ensembles were employed, the best final model was used for the final Docker container.

2.5   Inference and Postprocessing

The inference consists of the following steps:

1. Loading a given case.
2. Resampling the input case to $400 \times 400 \times 400$, clipping the intensity, and normalizing it to the [0–1] range.
3. Calculating the prediction (without thresholding).
4. Resampling the prediction by linear interpolation to the original shape and thresholding.
5. Performing the postprocessing based on the connected component analysis to leave only the largest connected component (for further meshing only).
6. Saving the calculated segmentation mask.

2.6   Meshing

The calculated segmentation mask is meshed using the Discrete Marching Cubes available in the VTK library. Afterward, the mesh is smoothed by WindowedSincPolyDataFilter with the following parameters for the surface meshing: (i) boundary smoothing set: false, (ii) feature edge smoothing set: false, (iii) number of iterations: 25, (iv) feature angle: 120, (v) pass band: 0.001, (vi) non-manifold smoothing: true. The following arguments are used for the mesh that was further used for volumetric meshing: (i) boundary smoothing set: true, (ii) feature edge smoothing set: true, (iii) number of iterations: 30, (iv) feature angle: 120, (v) pass band: 0.001, (vi) non-manifold smoothing: true. Moreover, all holes in the mesh are closed to make it watertight. Small branches are slightly extended by morphological operations (before meshing) to ensure that the Tet-Gen can create the volumetric mesh successfully.

2.7 Dataset

The training data consists of 56 annotated cases provided by the challenge organizers. The scan contains the aorta and all its branches acquired with the computed tomography angiography (CTA) [11,16,18]. The dataset, unlike other publicly available datasets, annotates the whole aortic vessel tree: the ascending aorta and the branches into the thoracic aorta, abdominal aorta, head/neck area, and iliac arteries branching to the legs. The cases were annotated using three datasets: KiTS [8,9], RIDER [31], and Dongyang Hospital. Several of the cases exhibit pathologies, such as aortic dissections or abdominal aortic aneurysms. The exemplary scans from each medical center are presented in Fig. 1. Only the data provided by the challenge organizers was used during training. No external data was used. No pretrained networks were used.

2.8 Experimental Setup

Apart from the final submission to the Grand Challenge platform, several ablation studies were performed to verify: (i) the influence of resampling to a lower resolution, (ii) the influence of cost function, and (iii) the impact of data augmentation. All these ablation studies were performed using a 5-fold cross-validation. All the performed experiments were trained until convergence. The hyperparameters for the final challenge submission are reported in Table 1.

Table 1. The training hyperparameters for the best-performing setup.

Parameter	Value
Initial learning rate:	0.001
Iteration size	64
Batch size	16
Decay rate	0.999
Cost function	Dice-Focal Loss
Max gradient value	2
Max gradient norm	10
Optimizer	AdamW
Optimizer weight decay	0.005
Volume resolution	$400 \times 400 \times 400$
Augmentation	Elastic, Affine, Contrast, Gaussian Noise
	Flipping, Motion Artifacts, Anisotropy

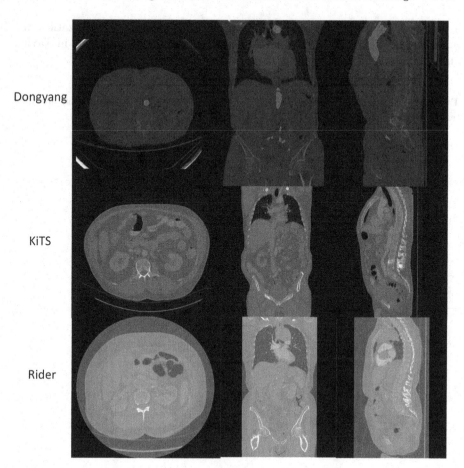

Fig. 1. Exemplary cases from each medical center. Please note the differences related to the intensity distributions (unrelated to the visualization window), field of view, and spatial resolution (e.g. Rider cases have significantly smaller voxel size).

2.9   Source Code

All network, training, augmentation, and inference hyperparameters are reported in the repository. The source code of the proposed contribution is available at [29]. The pretrained model is available upon request, as well as the access to the Grand Challenge algorithm [28].

3   Results

3.1   Aorta Segmentation

The results of aorta segmentation are evaluated using the Dice coefficient and the 95th percentile of the Hausdorff distance. The quantitative results for the

5-fold cross-validation are reported in Table 2 and qualitative visualizations are presented in Fig. 2. The results for the external test set are reported in Table 3 and compared to other challenge participants.

Table 2. The quantitative results on a 5-fold cross-validation (using the 56 provided training cases).

Method	Avg. DSC ↑	Avg. HD95 [mm] ↓
Ablation Studies - Resolution (Dice + Focal, full augmentation)		
400^3 (proposed)	0.9441	1.89
256^3	0.9235	2.45
224^3	0.9182	2.82
160^3	0.9081	3.56
Ablation Studies - Cost Function (400^3, full augmentation)		
Dice + Focal (proposed)	0.9441	1.89
Dice	0.9362	2.24
Dice + Cross-Entropy	0.9215	2.87
Focal	0.8748	5.59
Ablation Studies - Data Augmentation (400^3, Dice + Focal)		
Full Augmentation (proposed)	0.9441	1.89
Without Elastic	0.9331	2.37
Without Geometric	0.8941	3.42
Without Intensity	0.9417	2.14
No Augmentation	0.8872	3.51

The results present high stability in terms of both the Dice coefficient and Hausdorff Distance in the 5-fold cross validation. Moreover, they confirm the importance of data augmentation and maintaining high spatial resolution. Unfortunately, for two cases from the external test set the 95th percentile of HD is significantly higher (for all challenge participants). Since the test data is closed, it is impossible to determine what is the reason, namely whether it is connected to poor algorithm generalizability, the difficulty of particular cases (e.g. aorta dissections), or imperfect annotations.

3.2   Surface Meshing

Exemplary visualizations of the calculated surface meshes are presented in Fig. 3, next to the ground-truth meshes. It can be noted that the calculated meshes are of relatively high quality and the largest disagreements are within the small branches (which is expected). Figure 4 presents visualization for a case with exemplary aortic dissection for which the proposed method generalizes correctly.

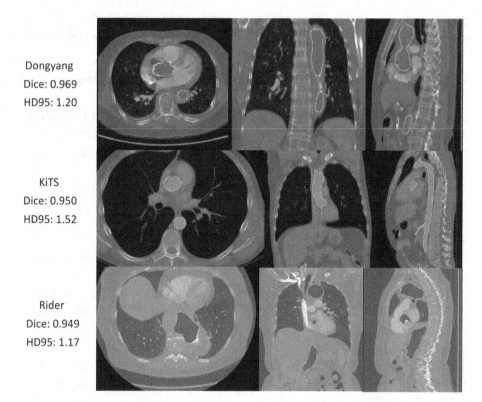

Dongyang
Dice: 0.969
HD95: 1.20

KiTS
Dice: 0.950
HD95: 1.52

Rider
Dice: 0.949
HD95: 1.17

Fig. 2. Exemplary visualizations from the internal validation set for cases from each data source. The ground-truths are shown in green and the calculated segmentation masks in red. (Color figure online)

The surface meshes were qualitatively evaluated by 8 clinical experts from 5 different hospitals located in Austria, Germany, Iran, and the United Kingdom. The experts evaluated two cases, one with the best quantitative scores, and one with the worst quantitative scores. They were asked to evaluate two aspects, the correctness of the model and the absence of artifacts. The results are presented in Table 4.

3.3   Volumetric Meshing

The quantitative results for the volumetric meshing are presented in Table 5. Unfortunately, due to the limitations of the Grand Challenge platform, the evaluation was based on the uploaded surface meshes, without the control of the volumetric meshing itself. The differences between participants in this subtask are rather minor and it is hard to conclude which method was the most appropriate, especially since the mesh correctness in terms of medical credibility was not evaluated, only the Jacobian-related statistics.

Table 3. The comparison of the proposed method to other top-performing SEG.A teams. Only the best submissions from each team are reported for the presentation clarity.

Team	Case A2C	Case A3C	Case A4C	Case A5C	Case A6C	Mean	Std
Dice Coefficient ↑							
Proposed	0.907	0.907	0.912	0.923	0.935	0.917	**0.012**
ATB	0.885	0.891	0.918	0.917	0.934	0.909	0.020
Brightskies	0.906	0.897	0.920	0.931	0.947	**0.920**	0.020
NVAUTO	0.887	0.889	0.923	0.928	0.947	0.915	0.025
TeamX	0.890	0.876	0.918	0.919	0.935	0.908	0.024
KARINA	0.895	0.895	0.919	0.928	0.944	0.916	0.021
Culrich	0.889	0.878	0.924	0.926	0.941	0.912	0.027
WGD	0.887	0.877	0.921	0.917	0.938	0.908	0.025
Ouradiology	0.883	0.862	0.911	0.916	0.936	0.902	0.029
95th percentile of HD [mm] ↓							
Proposed	13.50	6.95	2.92	2.48	1.88	5.55	4.88
ATB	10.38	7.99	2.61	2.38	1.88	5.05	3.88
Brightskies	13.25	11.79	2.61	2.23	1.59	6.30	5.71
NVAUTO	13.56	5.67	2.61	2.38	1.56	5.15	4.95
TeamX	13.19	10.24	2.83	3.00	2.00	6.25	5.11
KARINA	16.88	4.36	2.89	2.24	2.00	5.66	6.34
Culrich	15.59	7.53	2.65	2.23	2.00	6.00	5.82
WGD	11.70	7.09	3.01	3.42	1.88	5.42	4.01
Ouradiology	8.64	6.92	2.97	2.62	1.86	**4.61**	**2.99**

Table 4. Final results for the clinical evaluation based on the surface meshing. Correctness denotes the ranking in the amount of information that the calculated model correctly communicates to specialists while the absence ranks the resistance to segmentation artifacts.

Team	Correctness [rank] ↓	Absence [rank] ↓	Final Ranking ↓
Proposed	1	1	1
NVAUTO	1	2	2
Brightskies	3	3	3
Biomed	4	4	4
Cian	5	5	5

Table 5. The final results of the volumetric meshing task (Jac - Jacobian).

Team	Avg. Inv. Elements ↓	Median Jac ↑	Jac Variance ↓	Jac Skewness ↓	Final Ranking ↓
Biomed	3.49	0.570	$0.72 * 10^{-5}$	0.2446	1
NVAUTO	3.85	0.557	$0.79 * 10^{-5}$	0.2567	2
Proposed	4.55	0.550	$2.68 * 10^{-5}$	0.8667	3
Brightskies	5.98	0.545	$1.69 * 10^{-5}$	0.3324	4
Cian	61.76	−100	$> 10^3$	0.3651	5

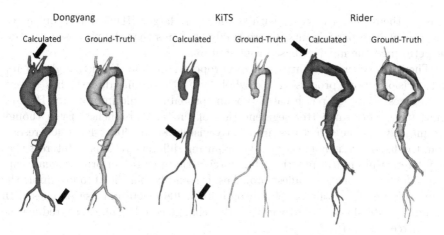

Fig. 3. Exemplary surface meshes for cases from all data sources (validation cases). Please note that the differences are mostly in fine-details related to small branches.

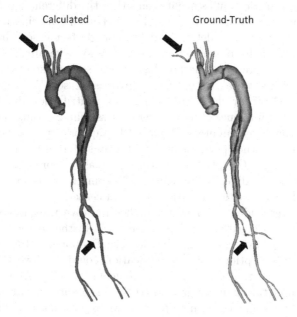

Fig. 4. Exemplary surface meshes for a case with an aortic dissection (Rider dataset - validation case). Note that the dissection was correctly segmented, the only differences are related to small branches.

4   Discussion

The overall outcomes of the proposed method are satisfactory. The method is the most stable in terms of the DC standard deviation among all SEG.A participants. The method achieved DC above 0.9 for all test cases and HD95 below 3mm for three of them. The two cases with significantly larger HD95 were problematic for all challenge participants. Interestingly, it seems that the proposed solution outperformed the nnUNet-based contributions.

There are several limitations of the proposed method. Even though our initial decision about processing the whole 3-D CT volume directly has several advantages, using the patch-based pipeline probably would improve the HD and allow us to perform better segmentation of the small branches. Even though the majority of the structures are clearly visible in the $400 \times 400 \times 400$ resolution, the fixed size is not resistant to acquiring different regions of interest that may happen in clinical practice, thus forcing the user to perform manual cropping. Moreover, for the smallest branches, it could be beneficial to upsample the input volumes to resolution far beyond $400 \times 400 \times 400$ and use patches with an appropriate shape. We expect that this change could significantly reduce the 95th percentile of HD.

Another limitation of the study itself is the size of the external test set. Unfortunately, just five testing cases make it relatively hard to compare our solution to other challenge participants since it seems that the differences between 7 top-performing teams are statistically insignificant. For all participating teams the median Dice and HD95 was determined by a single test case. Therefore, it is hard to draw any conclusions based on the quantitative results.

Nevertheless, the proposed method has several strong aspects. First, it provides a stable Dice score above 0.9 for all five test cases. With GPU support (which was turned off for the Grand Challenge contribution due to the platform limitation) the inference takes on average less than 2 s using NVIDIA A100 GPU and less than one minute without GPU support. It is a significant difference compared to other participants constantly suffering from the time limit strictly enforced in the GD platform (10 min per case). Moreover, the proposed method is resistant to different intensity and geometry variations, providing a useful tool in clinical practice in various medical centers.

There are several ideas on how to further improve the method. The first one is to transfer to a patch-based pipeline or to further extend the 3-D volume resolution (e.g. by employing libraries like DeepSpeed [19] to reduce the GPU memory consumption). Such modification could improve the segmentation of small branches that are crucial for medical credibility. Another idea to is perform the re-annotation of the ground-truth to separate aorta branches. Even though it would be a time-consuming process, we expect that it would result in a great improvement in small branches segmentation. Moreover, it would be interesting to check the influence of augmentation on methods outside the podium to measure the stability and generalizability, without influencing the final ranking. Finally, the volumetric meshing could be potentially improved by using novel deep learning-based solutions like FlexiCubes [23]. However, submission using a different volumetric meshing algorithm would require improvements to the Grand Challenge platform.

To conclude, we proposed a stable and robust method for automatic aorta segmentation. The method achieved competitive results in the SEG.A challenge and after minor improvements could potentially provide even better results. The source code is publicly available, as well as the model used for the final submission.

Acknowledgements. We gratefully acknowledge Polish HPC infrastructure PLGrid support within computational grant no. PLG/2023/016239.

References

1. SEGA Challenge. https://multicenteraorta.grand-challenge.org/multicenteraorta/ (2023). Accessed 29 Aug 2023
2. Berhane, H., et al.: Fully automated 3D aortic segmentation of 4D flow MRI for hemodynamic analysis using deep learning. Magn Reson Med. **84**, 2204–2218 (2020). https://doi.org/10.1002/mrm.28257
3. Cao, Y., et al.: Aortic dissection: identification of entry site with CT virtual intravascular endoscopy. Biomed. Imaging Interv. J. **6**(3), 1–7 (2010)
4. Cardoso, M.J., et al.: MONAI: an open-source framework for deep learning in healthcare (2022)
5. Chen, D., et al.: Multi-stage learning for segmentation of aortic dissections using a prior aortic anatomy simplification. Med. Image Anal. **69**, 101931 (2021). https://doi.org/10.1016/j.media.2020.101931
6. Fantazzini, A., et al.: 3D automatic segmentation of aortic computed tomography angiography combining multi-view 2d convolutional neural networks. Cardiovasc. Eng. Technol. **11**, 576–586 (2020). https://doi.org/10.1007/s13239-020-00481-z
7. Hahn, L., et al.: CT-based true- and false-lumen segmentation in type b aortic dissection using machine learning. Radiol. Cardiothorac. Imaging. **2**, e190179 (2020). https://doi.org/10.1148/ryct.2020190179
8. Heller, N., et al.: The KiTS19 Challenge Data: 300 Kidney Tumor Cases with Clinical Context, CT Semantic Segmentations, and Surgical Outcomes (2020). https://arxiv.org/abs/1904.00445
9. Heller, N., et al.: The state of the art in kidney and kidney tumor segmentation in contrast-enhanced CT imaging: results of the kits19 challenge. Med. Image Anal. **67**, 101821 (2021)
10. Howard, J.P., et al.: Automated analysis and detection of abnormalities in transaxial anatomical cardiovascular magnetic resonance images: a proof of concept study with potential to optimize image acquisition. Int. J. Cardiovasc. Imaging. **37**, 1033–1042 (2020). https://doi.org/10.1007/s10554-020-02050-w
11. Jin, Y., et al.: AI-based aortic vessel tree segmentation for cardiovascular diseases treatment: status quo. arXiv (2023). https://arxiv.org/abs/2108.02998
12. Jin, Y., et al.: Deep learning and particle filter-based aortic dissection vessel tree segmentation. In: Medical Imaging 2021: Biomedical Applications in Molecular, Structural, and Functional Imaging, p. 6. International Society for Optics and Photonics (2021)
13. Litjens, G., et al.: A survey on deep learning in medical image analysis. Med. Image Anal. **42**, 60–88 (2017)
14. López-Linares, K., et al.: Fully automatic detection and segmentation of abdominal aortic thrombus in post-operative CTA images using Deep Convolutional Neural Networks. Med. Image Anal. **46**, 202–214 (2018)

15. Nienaber, C.A., et al.: Endovascular repair of type B aortic dissection: long-term results of the randomized investigation of stent grafts in aortic dissection trial. Circ. Cardiovasc. Interven. **6**(4), 407–416 (2013)
16. Pepe, A., et al.: Detection, segmentation, simulation and visualization of aortic dissections: a review. Med. Image Anal. **65**, 101773 (2020)
17. Pérez-García, F., Sparks, R., Ourselin, S.: TorchIO: a python library for efficient loading, preprocessing, augmentation and patch-based sampling of medical images in deep learning. Comput. Methods Programs Biomed. **208**, 106236 (2021). https://doi.org/10.1016/j.cmpb.2021.106236
18. Radl, L., et al.: AVT: multicenter aortic vessel tree CTA dataset collection with ground truth segmentation masks. Data Brief **40**, 107801 (2022)
19. Rasley, J., Rajbhandari, S., Ruwase, O., He, Y.: DeepSpeed: system optimizations enable training deep learning models with over 100 billion parameters. In: 26th ACM SIGKDD International Conference on Knowledge Discovery & Data Mining, pp. 3505–3506 (2020). https://doi.org/10.1145/3394486.3406703
20. Ronneberger, O., Fischer, P., Brox, T.: U-net: convolutional networks for biomedical image segmentation. In: Navab, N., Hornegger, J., Wells, W.M., Frangi, A.F. (eds.) MICCAI 2015. LNCS, vol. 9351, pp. 234–241. Springer, Cham (2015). https://doi.org/10.1007/978-3-319-24574-4_28
21. Shahzad, R., et al.: Automated extraction and labelling of the arterial tree from whole-body MRA data. Med. Image Anal. **24**(1), 28–40 (2015). https://doi.org/10.1016/j.media.2015.05.008
22. Shamshad, F., et al.: Transformers in medical imaging: a survey. Med. Image Anal. **88**, 102802 (2023)
23. Shen, T., et al.: Flexible isosurface extraction for gradient-based mesh optimization. ACM Trans. Graph. **42**(4), 1–6 (2023). https://doi.org/10.1145/3592430
24. Sieren, M.M., et al.: Automated segmentation and quantification of the healthy and diseased aorta in CT angiographies using a dedicated deep learning approach. Eur. Radiol. **32**, 690–701 (2022). https://doi.org/10.1007/s00330-021-08130-2
25. Tortora, G.J., Nielsen, M.T.: Principles of Human Anatomy, 14th edn. Wiley, New York (2016)
26. Trullo, R., et al.: Segmentation of organs at risk in thoracic CT images using a SharpMask architecture and conditional random fields. pp. 1003–1006. IEEE Computer Society (2017). https://doi.org/10.1109/ISBI.2017.7950685
27. Varoquaux, G., Cheplygina, V.: Machine learning for medical imaging: methodological failures and recommendations for the future. NPJ Digit. Med. **5**(1), 48 (2022)
28. Wodzinski, M.: SEGA Algorithm. https://grand-challenge.org/algorithms/sega_mw/ (2023). Accessed 29 Aug 2023
29. Wodzinski, M.: SEGA Code Repository (2023). https://github.com/MWod/SEGA_MW_2023. Accessed 29 Aug 2023
30. Yu, Y., et al.: A three-dimensional deep convolutional neural network for automatic segmentation and diameter measurement of type B aortic dissection. Korean J. Radiol. **22**, 168–178 (2021). https://doi.org/10.3348/kjr.2020.0313
31. Zhao, B., Schwartz, L.H., Kris, M.G.: Data from Rider Lung CT. The Cancer Imaging Archive. TCIA (2015)
32. Zhong, J., et al.: Segmentation of the thoracic aorta using an attention-gated u-net, vol. 11597, pp. 147–153. International Society for Optics and Photonics, SPIE (2021). https://doi.org/10.1117/12.2581947

Position-Encoded Pixel-to-Prototype Contrastive Learning for Aortic Vessel Tree Segmentation

Hyeongyu Kim[1], Yejee Shin[1,2], and Dosik Hwang[1,3,4,5](✉)

[1] School of Electrical and Electronic Engineering, Yonsei University, Seoul, Republic of Korea
dosik.hwang@yonsei.ac.kr
[2] Probe Medical, Seoul, Republic of Korea
[3] Department of Radiology and Center for Clinical Imaging Data Science, Yonsei University, Seoul, Republic of Korea
[4] Department of Oral and Maxillofacial Radiology, College of Dentistry, Yonsei University, Seoul, Republic of Korea
[5] Center for Healthcare Robotics, Korea Institute of Science and Technology, Seoul, Republic of Korea

Abstract. The SegA challenge concentrates on segmenting the aorta in CTA scans. Our approach is divided into two main phases: a broad, preliminary segmentation to identify the aorta's general vicinity, and a subsequent detailed segmentation for precision. The distinguishing feature of our method is the use of prototype-based learning during the detailed segmentation. By studying specific examples from the foreground, the algorithm captures the nuanced differences in aortic structures, leading to more precise segmentation results. Our technique demonstrated its robustness by achieving the 5th rank in the phase 2 of the challenge. Such advancements in segmentation techniques not only prove effective in competitions but also have the potential to revolutionize medical image analysis, paving the way for improved diagnostic and treatment planning in the clinical realm.

Keywords: Aorta segmentation · Medical image segmentation

1 Introduction

Accurate aorta segmentation holds paramount significance within the realm of medical image analysis and clinical practice. The aorta, as the largest artery in the human body, plays a pivotal role in transporting oxygenated blood from the heart to various organs. Precise segmentation of the aorta from medical images, such as CT scans and MRI scans, has multifaceted implications that span across diagnostics, treatment planning, and research endeavors [2,3,6].

A. Pepe et al. (Eds.): SEGA 2023, LNCS 14539, pp. 55–66, 2024.
https://doi.org/10.1007/978-3-031-53241-2_5

The importance of accurate aorta segmentation becomes evident in its critical role in clinical diagnostics and disease assessment [4]. Various cardiovascular conditions, including aneurysms and aortic dissections, can be accurately diagnosed and monitored through precise aorta segmentation. Early detection of aneurysms is crucial as it allows clinicians to monitor their growth and plan interventions before the risk of rupture escalates. Similarly, aortic dissections and congenital abnormalities can be identified and evaluated with precision through segmented images. Accurate aorta segmentation is pivotal for treatment planning and interventions. It guides surgical precision by determining optimal locations, sizes, and approaches for aortic procedures, thus minimizing risks and improving outcomes. This precision also forms the basis for patient-specific modeling, revolutionizing cardiovascular care through simulated surgeries that enhance overall surgical strategies.

Furthermore, accurate segmentation's significance extends to research and treatment innovation in cardiovascular medicine. Researchers leverage precise segmentation to analyze blood flow patterns, explore biomechanical factors, and develop improved treatment approaches. Post-intervention, accurate segmentation aids in monitoring patient progress and treatment effectiveness, allowing timely adjustments to care plans. In conclusion, accurate aorta segmentation's multifaceted contributions are integral to refining medical practices, enhancing research, and ultimately advancing patient care.

However, the traditional methods which often require manual intervention by medical experts, are not only time-consuming but also prone to human errors. Moreover, the manual delineation of aorta boundaries is labor-intensive and can lead to variations in results across different practitioners. This variability in manual segmentation further underscores the need for automated and accurate segmentation techniques.

With the advancement of deep learning, automatic aorta segmentation has reached a considerably conquerable level [1,8,9,12,15]. However, due to the unique characteristics of the thin and elongated aorta, achieving a consistently reliable stage of segmentation remains imperfect, missing some detailed and fine segmentation at the end of the aortic tree.

nnU-Net [7], which has become the standard platform for medical image segmentation these days with its subsequent families [17], provides a strong baseline for almost all modalities of medical imaging with various targets, including aorta segmentation on CTA scans. However, even with the strong baselines, conducting accurate and exact medical image segmentation in one single step is quite challenging task, especially for the vessel tree segmentation task such as aorta where the targets consist of both very thick and thin trees. Therefore, there still exists room for performance improvement, by modifying it to fit best for the aorta segmentation.

nnU-Net and its families adopt patch-crop-based methods with sliding-window-based prediction to limit the FOV and achieve the finest segmentation at the same time. However, even this method has several shortcomings, such as long inference time and performance dependency on FOV and patch settings. To overcome those, our methods consist of two stages based on this strong baseline, for the finest aorta segmentation, where a coarse segmentation network for initialization is followed by a prototype-based fine segmentation network.

Through the modification of the baseline to our framework, we accomplished 5th in the phase 2 leaderboard, while showing the validity of our structure design and proving the strong performance of our network. Throughout the paper, we will analyze the task and the situation, and describe how we designed our methods with comparative results.

2   Problem Definition

The objective of the challenge is to conduct AVT segmentation with the model trained on data from three institutions, and testing it on data from the fourth institution. Therefore, ensuring the robustness and stability of a model is an important issue. Another consideration was the hardware. Due to the computational resource limitations of the platform used for the challenge operation, the participants were necessitated to consider those limitations in their network design paradigms. However, those limitations were on the conflicting side with the nature of nnU-Net, where patch-crop-based inference with sliding window naturally led to increased repetition of inference with increased time. Increasing the patch size to reduce the number of inferences was also now possible due to vRAM limitations. Therefore, we focused on building as efficient a network as possible to best maximize the resources available while increasing the segmentation performance. Our framework was built upon that principle.

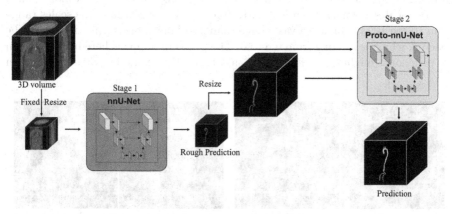

Fig. 1. Overview of our proposed framework.

3 Methods

3.1 Framework

Our overall framework leverages most of the settings in the nnU-Net framework. As shown in Fig. 1., two nnU-Net architectures are cascaded.

3.2 First Stage: Coarse Segmentation

In the first stage, for efficiency, we deleted all information from the data including pixel spacing and orientation, and resized it to small sizes of volumes. This is because we empirically found out that abstract segmentation is possible enough even when completely absent from such information, even though the fine segmentation performance depends on such settings. Due to the patch-crop-wise training and sliding-window nature of the nnU-Net, selecting patch size and overlap ratio between patches led to significant differences in the inference time. Therefore, we fixed the resized image size to ($z \times 224 \times 224$), with the patch crop size to ($120, 224, 224$). This saved to 4x faster inference time, with 5–10% DSC drop when compared to the initial nnU-Net settings, which are enough for the first stage with coarse segmentation, as we planned.

3.3 Second Stage: Fine Segmentation

Spacing Control and Preprocessing. To conduct fine and accurate segmentation, we now control spacing and sizes differently from the first stage, which is important processing for medical images [14]. Here, we designed those parts based on the statistics shown in the training dataset. Within all training data from three institutions, we found that when seeing the dataset in axial plane, x-y axis scales are fixed from 512×512 to 620×620, whereas z-axis scales range from 100 to 1024, which is a vast range than xy-plane. This is consistent with the spacing, which is ranging from 0.6 to 6. The problem happens here because when we pick some median spacing values as targets. For example, when the median

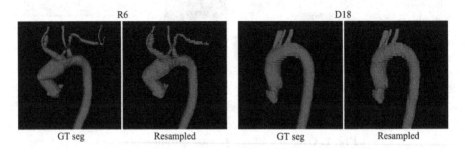

Fig. 2. Artifact pattern with different spacing. When prediction is conducted with fixed spacing, the volumes should be resized to fit the fixed target spacing and should be re-sampled back to its original spacing after the model run. In this process, there exists an artifact according to its interpolation methods.

spacing was 3, the spacing $6 \rightarrow 3 \rightarrow 6$ case leads to prediction on interpolated and sampled back again, with no problem, whereas spacing $0.5 \rightarrow 3 \rightarrow 0.5$ case leads to inaccurate interpolation problem, which leads to impaired predictions, as shown in Fig. 2. Reducing the target spacing can remedy this, but increases the computational burden, which is an important tradeoff to overcome. Therefore, we took 75% ratio of z-plane spacing and took 50% value from the x-y plane, which becomes [1.4 0.68 0.68] for z, y, x each. And taking the first stage output as an input to the second stage and increasing efficiency, we limit the FOV of the entire volume. We crop the volumes depending on the first stage segmentation results and match it back after the second stage.

Cascaded Conditional Training. To best utilize the first stage output as a segmentation guidance, we take its output as an input to the second stage. However, end-to-end training takes so much computational resources during training with increased time, with less stability and difficult training. Therefore, we conducted this with separated processes. In this setting, we need to simulate the predictions from the first stage, as its prediction may be in a wide range, missing some fine trees of the aorta. To ensure the stability, we planned the input as below:

$$\hat{y}_1 = \begin{cases} e(y,r) & \text{if } 0.6 \leq p, \\ d(y,r) & \text{if } 0.2 < p \leq 0.6, \\ y & \text{if } 0.1 < p \leq 0.2, \\ 0 & \text{if } p \leq 0.1. \end{cases}$$

where p is a uniform random variable from $0 \leq p \leq 1$, e and d stands for each erosion and dilation with the kernel of the radius of r, with r from $0.5 \leq r \leq 3$, randomly selected. Through this strategy, the second stage of training can achieve stabilized and accurate inference when the first stage prediction is fed.

Prototype-Based Learning. Inside the entire volume of the AVT, there exist varying characteristics depending on its spatial locations. Although those share common features regarding the aorta, there also exist differences including surrounding organs, thicknesses, or splitting properties. Considering that the nnU-Net framework is conducting its segmentation, these differences may not be considered enough and may miss some. To overcome this, we conducted two additional strategies, which can be comprised together as (1) positional encoded and (2) prototype based learning. As referring to [18], we suppose that the features from different locations share different characteristics, therefore train those based on its clustered prototypes. We used PPC (Pixel-to-prototype contrastive) based loss with online clustering and prototype updated [5].

Considering the variance in voxel features from the Aorta based on position, we employ the K-means clustering algorithm [11], focusing solely on the position information corresponding to each voxel feature. This positional-based clustering ensures that no cluster has an inherent bias towards any specific point.

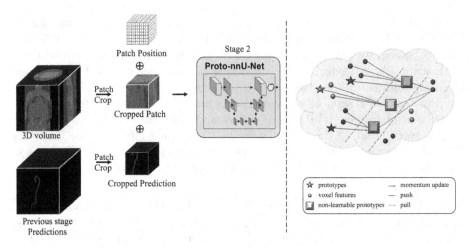

Fig. 3. We added two extra parts to the nnU-Net framework. First, to distinguish the cropped patch location, we added positional encoding to the cropped voxel. And with the first stage output, prototype-based learning is conducted. At the last stage of the nnU-Net decoder, we use pixel embedding to get prototypes of a batch and update the global prototypes in an exponential-moving-average method. The pixel embedding is updated with PPC-type pixel to prototype contrastive loss, where pulled to the closest prototype and pushed to the others. In this way, even within the same AVT, pixel embedding of different features regarding spatial location or surroundings can be trained differently in an effective way.

To integrate K-means clustering into our methodology, we select voxel features z produced just before the final layer, which can be represented as:

$$z^{(h,w,d)} = h_\theta(x), \tag{1}$$

Where $z^{(h,w,d)}$ refers to the voxel features, x is the input image from the CT scan, and $h_\theta(.)$ designates the baseline model, such as ResU-Net. The differentiation of these features into foreground (aorta region) and background is captured by:

$$z_f^{(h,w,d)}, z_b^{(h,w,d)} = g(z^{(h,w,d)}), \tag{2}$$

The function $g(.)$ assists in isolating foreground features, which solely comprise aorta features, from background features. The prototype, corresponding to the c classes, is then defined as:

$$q^c = Kmeans(z_f^{(h,w,d)}, h, w, d), \tag{3}$$

To capture a broader swath of instance information, our strategy leverages a memory bank for dynamic prototype updates, governed by momentum.

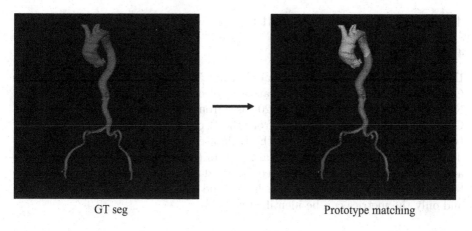

GT seg   Prototype matching

Fig. 4. Visualization of the learned prototypes. We trained our model with fixed number of prototypes (c = 5), but the prototype-pixel matched result shows that only three prototypes were actively used during the learning process. Nevertheless, the result shows that discriminative patterns of AVT are distinguished with our method.

As depicted in Fig. 3, this momentum-driven paradigm ensures that each prototype's evolution is predicated upon its proximity to features resident within the memory bank:

$$q^{c,m} = m(q^c), \tag{4}$$

Here, $q^{c,m}$ symbolizes the regularized prototypes, reflecting a diverse ensemble of instance features.

Within the framework of contrastive representation learning, each positive pair is composed of an instance and its corresponding semantic prototype. Conversely, negative pairs emerge by pairing instances with non-correlated semantic prototypes. Adhering to this pairing strategy and given a positive pair (z, c), we integrate the ProtoNCE loss. Based on the prototype InfoNCE loss [10,13] formulation, it is:

$$L_{ProtoNCE} = -\log \frac{\exp(\langle z_f, q^{c,m} \rangle / \tau)}{\sum_{c' \neq c} \exp(\langle z_f, q^{c',m} \rangle / \tau)}, \tag{5}$$

where $\langle .,. \rangle$ indicates the dot product, and τ serves as a temperature scaling parameter. This approach ensures an optimized representation of voxel features, enhancing the accuracy and clarity of our CT-based aorta segmentation.

As shown in Fig. 4, the automatically updated prototypes show different clustered centers based on its spatial locations, which indirectly indicates that training those pixels separately can better extract their features.

4 Experiment and Results

4.1 Setup

Dataset. Our method was evaluated using 56 CTA scans from the SEG.A. Challenge in 2023. The SEG.A. dataset [16] consists of three institutions: the KiTS Grand Challenge (featuring 20 cases from the K dataset), the Rider Lung CT dataset (comprising 18 cases from the R dataset), and Dongyang Hospital (which contributed 18 cases from the D dataset). From this collection, We randomly selected 48 cases of the total subjects (57 subjects) to use for training, and data from 9 subjects were used for validation. There were two phases for testing in this challenge, where each two and five hidden cases were provided and only the metrics can be identified (Fig. 5).

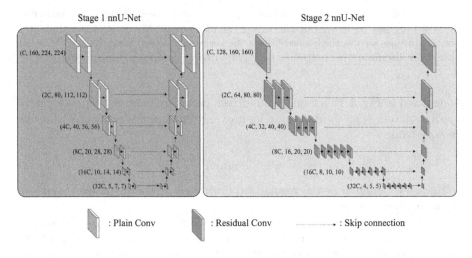

Fig. 5. Network architecture for both stages. We hold C- = 32 for the same and manage the encoder depth. Stage 2 used residual Conv blocks, where the input and output are connected with residual connection, which is omitted in the visualization. Stage 1 takes the entire volume as an input, whereas stage 2 takes cropped patches of the volumes.

Metrics. The ranking was measured by taking the average of all rankings from each four metrics, which are 1. HD 50pc, 2. HD std, 3. DSC 50pc, 4. DSC std.

HD 50pc & DSC 50pc. It takes the 50% position Hausdorff distance (HD) and DSC as representative metrics, which corresponds to the median value. Considering that there were only five test cases, this becomes the third-lowest HD value with the third-highest DSC values.

HD std & DSC std. The standard deviation of all Hausdorff distance values and DSC.

Implementation Details. We conducted a comprehensive evaluation of our proposed method, benchmarking it against a prominent existing approach, nnUNet. We used *Plain-Conv-UNet* for the first stage and *ResEnc-UNet* for the second stage. By changing the configuration, we set the model specifics as below:

The overall trainer parameters except for the patch size are same for the both stages, including an initial learning rate of 1e−2 with a weight decay of 3e−5, the number of iterations per epoch 250, with 1000 epochs. For the loss function, we used default DC with BCE loss.

4.2   Results

Ablation Studies. To compare the results between the baseline model and our prototype-based model, we compared some results of four versions, with different patch sizes with the inclusion of prototype-based learning. The results are from the internal validation set, which was separated from the training set from three institutions. As shown in Table 1, it shows that the combination of the prototype included a version with a larger patch size showed increased performance.

Table 1. Comparison in internal validation set. Larger patch size with prototype-included model showed the highest DSC.

	Patch size (80, 192, 192)	Patch size (160, 256, 256)
Baseline	0.9614	0.9557
With N = 5 Prototype	0.9604	**0.9640**

4.3   Leaderboard

In the table presented, our team secured the 5th position in the phase 2 leaderboard. Our scores were as follows: HD 50pc at 2.8284, HD std at 6.3396, DSC 50pc at 0.9188, and DSC std at 0.0209. Despite our 5th place ranking, barring the HD std, our performance was commendably close to that of the top-ranked team. Delving deeper into the specifics, our HD for the five test cases were 2.236, 1.828, 4.358, 2.0, and 16.881 respectively, averaging at 5.4606. The anomalous case of 16.881 notably skewed our standard deviation, placing us at the 25th rank for that metric. However, a comparative analysis with the 4th place team reveals that their HDs were 2.484, 2.918, 6.951, 1.876, and 13.506, averaging at 5.547. Despite our HD score being marginally lower, it's essential to acknowledge that the ranking in the challenge was significantly influenced by the uniformity of the results, which might have contributed to the disparity in rankings (Table 2).

Table 2. Results from the official leaderboard for Phase 2. Our team ranked 5th place, with 11 on the mean position.

	Team	Mean Position	HD 50pc (Position)	HD std (Position)	DSC 50pc (Position)	DSC std (Position)
1st	ATB	4.5	2.6125(1)	3.8819(3)	0.9173(9)	0.0204(5)
2nd	Brightskies	7.5	2.6125(3)	5.7166(20)	0.9205(4)	0.0197(3)
3rd	amrn	8	2.6125(1)	4.9506(12)	0.9234(3)	0.0260(16)
4th	IWM	9	2.9190(8)	4.8759(11)	0.9121(16)	0.0121(1)
5th	**KARINA** (ours)	11	2.8284(6)	6.3396(25)	0.9188(6)	0.0209(7)
5th	TeamX	11	3.0000(12)	5.1105(15)	0.9182(7)	0.0238(10)

5   Discussion

The endeavor to achieve precise segmentation of the aortic vessel tree (AVT) has been driven by the sheer clinical importance of the aorta in human physiology and medical diagnostics. Our study, in line with the aims of the SegA challenge, underscores the efficacy of a two-step segmentation approach in the realm of Computed Tomography Angiography (CTA) scans, emphasizing the amalgamation of coarse and fine segmentation methodologies.

From the outset, the coarse segmentation played a pivotal role in setting the stage for more intricate delineation processes. By providing an initial estimation of the aorta's position, it not only localized the region of interest but also ensured that the subsequent fine segmentation could be more focused, and therefore, more accurate. This layered approach mirrors the broader principles in medical diagnostics - where a general understanding precedes more intricate examinations.

Our primary innovation was centered on the fine segmentation process, where the concept of Prototype-based learning was introduced. By harnessing multiple prototypes derived from foreground pixels, the methodology transcends traditional deep learning approaches. Instead of merely relying on pixel intensity values or convolutional filters, the algorithm learns from these prototypes, thereby gaining nuanced insights into the varying structures of the aorta. This approach, in essence, mimics the cognitive processes of medical experts, who draw upon their vast repository of prior cases to inform their current diagnostic decisions.

The results from the SegA challenge are a testament to the robustness of this methodology. Achieving the 5th position in a competitive landscape reaffirms the potential of Prototype-based learning in medical imaging.

However, it's essential to contextualize these findings within the broader challenges of aorta segmentation. As highlighted in the introduction, the complexities of the aorta, given its thin and elongated nature, pose unique challenges. While our methodology has shown commendable success, the end regions of the aortic tree still present obstacles that need further research. Traditional methods, with their reliance on manual intervention, underscore the critical need for automated solutions. Yet, achieving perfection in segmentation, especially in the terminal regions of the aorta, remains an ongoing challenge.

6   Conclusion

Our study presented a novel approach to the intricate task of aortic vessel tree segmentation, underlining the potential of Prototype-based learning in the realm of medical image analysis. The two-phase strategy, which distinctly delineates the aorta, holds promise for transformative advancements in clinical diagnostics. The significant achievement in the SegA challenge, particularly the commendable ranking on the leaderboard, affirms the robustness of our method. As the complexities of medical image segmentation continue to challenge the healthcare sector, methodologies such as ours stand out, offering a beacon of hope for improved patient care and diagnosis. Looking ahead, we anticipate our innovative techniques will set new standards, driving the next wave of breakthroughs in medical imaging.

Acknowledgements. This research was supported by Basic Science Research Program through the National Research Foundation of Korea funded by the Ministry of Science and ICT (2021R1A4A1031437, 2022R1A2C2008983, 2021R1C1C2008773), Artificial Intelligence Graduate School Program at Yonsei University [No. 2020-0-01361], the KIST Institutional Program (Project No.2E32271-23-078), and partially supported by the Yonsei Signature Research Cluster Program of 2023 (2023-22-0008).

References

1. Berhane, H., et al.: Fully automated 3d aortic segmentation of 4d flow MRI for hemodynamic analysis using deep learning. Magn. Reson. Med. **84**(4), 2204–2218 (2020)
2. Choke, E., et al.: A review of biological factors implicated in abdominal aortic aneurysm rupture. Eur. J. Vasc. Endovasc. Surg. **30**(3), 227–244 (2005)
3. Comelli, A., et al.: Deep learning approach for the segmentation of aneurysmal ascending aorta. Biomed. Eng. Lett. **11**, 15–24 (2021)
4. Deng, X., Zheng, Y., Xu, Y., Xi, X., Li, N., Yin, Y.: Graph cut based automatic aorta segmentation with an adaptive smoothness constraint in 3d abdominal CT images. Neurocomputing **310**, 46–58 (2018)
5. Du, Y., Fu, Z., Liu, Q., Wang, Y.: Weakly supervised semantic segmentation by pixel-to-prototype contrast. In: Proceedings of the IEEE/CVF Conference on Computer Vision and Pattern Recognition, pp. 4320–4329 (2022)
6. Graffy, P.M., Liu, J., O'Connor, S., Summers, R.M., Pickhardt, P.J.: Automated segmentation and quantification of aortic calcification at abdominal CT: application of a deep learning-based algorithm to a longitudinal screening cohort. Abdom. Radiol. **44**, 2921–2928 (2019)
7. Isensee, F., Jaeger, P.F., Kohl, S.A., Petersen, J., Maier-Hein, K.H.: nnU-Net: a self-configuring method for deep learning-based biomedical image segmentation. Nat. Methods **18**(2), 203–211 (2021)

8. Jin, Q., Meng, Z., Pham, T.D., Chen, Q., Wei, L., Su, R.: DUNet: a deformable network for retinal vessel segmentation. Knowl.-Based Syst. **178**, 149–162 (2019)
9. Jin, Y., et al.: AI-based aortic vessel tree segmentation for cardiovascular diseases treatment: status quo. arXiv preprint arXiv:2108.02998 (2021)
10. Li, J., Zhou, P., Xiong, C., Hoi, S.C.: Prototypical contrastive learning of unsupervised representations. arXiv preprint arXiv:2005.04966 (2020)
11. Lloyd, S.: Least squares quantization in PCM. IEEE Trans. Inf. Theory **28**(2), 129–137 (1982)
12. Moccia, S., De Momi, E., El Hadji, S., Mattos, L.S.: Blood vessel segmentation algorithms-review of methods, datasets and evaluation metrics. Comput. Methods Programs Biomed. **158**, 71–91 (2018)
13. Oord, A.v.d., Li, Y., Vinyals, O.: Representation learning with contrastive predictive coding. arXiv preprint arXiv:1807.03748 (2018)
14. Park, D., et al.: Importance of CT image normalization in radiomics analysis: prediction of 3-year recurrence-free survival in non-small cell lung cancer. Eur. Radiol. **32**(12), 8716–8725 (2022)
15. Pepe, A., et al.: Detection, segmentation, simulation and visualization of aortic dissections: a review. Med. Image Anal. **65**, 101773 (2020)
16. Radl, L., et al.: AVT: Multicenter aortic vessel tree CTA dataset collection with ground truth segmentation masks. Data Brief **40**, 107801 (2022)
17. Zhou, H.Y., Guo, J., Zhang, Y., Yu, L., Wang, L., Yu, Y.: nnFormer: interleaved transformer for volumetric segmentation. arXiv preprint arXiv:2109.03201 (2021)
18. Zhou, T., Wang, W., Konukoglu, E., Van Gool, L.: Rethinking semantic segmentation: a prototype view. In: Proceedings of the IEEE/CVF Conference on Computer Vision and Pattern Recognition, pp. 2582–2593 (2022)

Misclassification Loss for Segmentation of the Aortic Vessel Tree

Abbas Khan[1,2], Muhammad Asad[3], Alexander Zolotarev[2,4], Caroline Roney[2,4], Anthony Mathur[6], Martin Benning[2,5], and Gregory Slabaugh[1,2(✉)]

[1] School of Electronic Engineering and Computer Science, Queen Mary University of London, London, UK
g.slabaugh@qmul.ac.uk
[2] Queen Mary's Digital Environment Research Institute, London, UK
[3] School of Biomedical Engineering and Imaging Sciences, King's College London, London, UK
[4] School of Engineering and Materials Science, Queen Mary University of London, London, UK
[5] School of Mathematical Sciences, Queen Mary University of London, London, UK
[6] Centre for Cardiovascular Medicine and Devices, William Harvey Research Institute, Queen Mary University of London, London, UK

Abstract. Common pixel-based loss functions for image segmentation struggle with the fine-scale structures often found in the aortic vessel tree. In this paper, we propose a Misclassification Loss (MC loss) function, which can effectively suppress false positives and rescue the false negatives. A differentiable eXclusive OR (XOR) operation is implemented to identify these false predictions, which are then minimized through a cross-entropy loss. The proposed MC loss helps the network achieve better performance by focusing on these difficult regions. On the Segmentation of the Aorta SEG.A. 2023 challenge, our method achieves a Dice score of 0.93 and a Hausdorff Distance (HD) of 3.50 mm on a 5-fold split of 56 training subjects. We participated in the SEG.A. 2023 challenge, and the proposed method ranks among the top-six approaches in the validation phase-1. The pre-trained models, source code, and implementation will be made public.

Keywords: Segmentation · Aortic vessel trees · False Prediction Loss function for segmentation

1 Introduction

The heart supplies blood to all body parts through the aorta, which is an important anatomy for cardiovascular disease diagnosis. Aortic disorders are considered a significant cause of death for heart patients [15]. The initial screening of the aorta and all its related branches, collectively known as the aortic vessel tree (AVT), is performed using computed tomography (CT). To monitor the diseases associated with the aorta, the AVT structure is identified, and changes are

A. Pepe et al. (Eds.): SEGA 2023, LNCS 14539, pp. 67–79, 2024.
https://doi.org/10.1007/978-3-031-53241-2_6

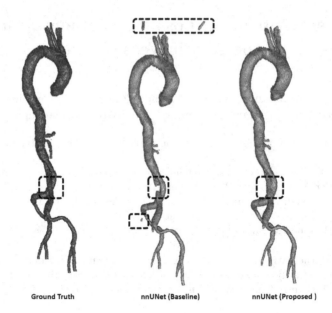

Ground Truth   nnUNet (Baseline)   nnUNet (Proposed)

Fig. 1. Visual comparison of our proposed approach (a) Ground Truth (b) Segmentation from nnUNet trained on a Dice cross-entropy loss, and (c) Segmentation from our proposed approach. Please zoom in for details.

analyzed over time [13]. However, manual reconstruction of the AVT is a cumbersome and time-consuming task for clinicians. To overcome these difficulties, the Segmentation of the Aorta SEG.A. 2023 challenge[1] was proposed for bringing automated AI-based aorta segmentation methods into clinical practice [18].

Related Work. In this section, we briefly describe key approaches that utilize deep learning to segment the aorta. A cascaded two-stage convolutional neural network CNN-based approach is proposed by [14] to segment both the aorta and the true lumen. The CNNs extract features from the whole aortic lumen and true lumen, while the false lumen is reconstructed via a post-processing step. Cao et al. [3] proposed a serial multi-task model to segment the whole aorta, true lumen and false lumen. Both networks are 3D and use down-sampled images of size 128 × 128 × 256 to reduce computational complexity. Another multi-stage network is proposed by [5], where the first CNN coarsely segments the aorta, followed by three single-view CNNs to fine-segment the aorta along the axial, sagittal, and coronal planes. Finally, multi-view integration is performed to merge the predictions.

Segmentation of fine-scale structures is a challenging problem and is being addressed by many researchers. For example, clDice [23] finds the skeleton over the likelihood map. TopoNet [11] is based on persistent homology [4]; the identified erroneous predicted points from the likelihood map are re-weighted in the

---

[1] https://multicenteraorta.grand-challenge.org/.

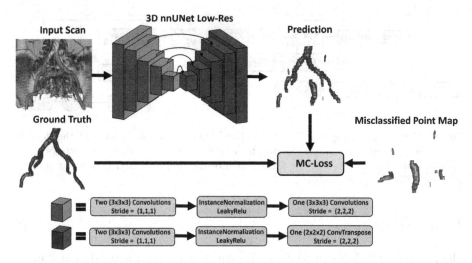

Fig. 2. Overview of our method. The proposed Misclassification (MC) Loss identifies the false positives and false negatives (misclassified points map). The MC Loss is defined based on this misclassified points map. Please zoom in for details.

training loss. This method generated many irrelevant points and became very expensive in terms of training. DMT loss [9] is another skeleton-based loss and uses discrete Morse theory to find skeletons and related patches. Agata et al. [16] trained both UNet [22] and pre-trained VVG-16 [24] iteratively to produce progressive refinements. The homotopy warping loss [10] uses distance transforms to find incorrect predictions and then incorporates them into the training to further refine the segmentation.

In this paper, we propose a plug-and-play loss function, which uses a simple yet effective approach to find falsely predicted voxels (false positives and false negatives). A differentiable XOR-gate is implemented between predicted foreground voxels and ground truth to find all points where the network predicts wrong voxels, i.e. false positives and false negatives collectively producing a *misclassified points map (MPM)*. As a second step, we map these points to the output logits and then fine-tune the segmentation network on misclassified voxels. The MC loss is meant to be used in conjunction with another loss (in our case, the Dice cross-entropy loss) that encourages true predictions (i.e. true positives and true negatives). It is therefore important to balance the MC loss and the original loss. When properly balanced, the MC loss can effectively remove the false positives and retrieve false negatives, as shown in Fig. 1 compared to the original loss.

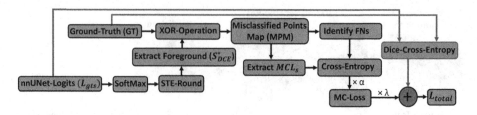

Fig. 3. Flowchart of proposed MC Loss. The blue color arrows represent the flow of Dice cross-entropy loss which is the first term of Eq. 1, and the black color arrows show the different steps involved in the formulation of the proposed MC Loss (second term of Eq. 1). (Color figure online)

2   Methods

The proposed MC loss can be used with any segmentation network; Fig. 2 illustrates the overall idea of incorporating it in an nnUNet network. The explanation of computing the proposed MC-loss is shown in Fig. 3.

By identifying the misclassified voxels (false positives and false negatives) from the predictions of a trained segmentation network, we can fine-tune the same network by penalizing the misclassified voxels. This fine-tuning stage will reduce the model's errors without impairing the true positives and true negatives.

As a first step, we trained a nnUNet [12] with a combined Dice cross-entropy loss (L_{DCE}) to generate the initial segmentation map. As a second stage of training, we use the weights of this trained nnUNet and penalize it with the sum of L_{DCE} and proposed misclassification loss (L_{MC}), i.e.

$$L_{total} = L_{DCE} + \lambda \cdot L_{MC} \tag{1}$$

where λ is a positive balancing factor influencing the effect of two losses. A very high λ will force the network solely to focus on difficult points and misclassify the easy voxels already segmented in the first stage. A very low value of λ will not affect the second-stage training, and the network will retain its previous weights. Here, we argue that the value of λ varies from dataset to dataset and for the SEG.A. data we used $\lambda = 5\mathrm{e}{-06}$. A detailed ablation study for choosing this balancing factor is provided in Sect. 3.1.

2.1   nnUNet Architecture

We use a 3D low-res nnUNet [12] network with $128 \times 128 \times 128$ input dimensions, as shown in Fig. 2. The maximum number of features is set to 320, and two convolutional layers with a filter size of $3 \times 3 \times 3$ were used at each stage of the encoder and decoder. Instance normalization and leaky Relu follow each convolution layer. Skip connections are employed at each encoder stage for better back-propagation of gradients. The features are downsampled with a convolution stride of 2 at the encoder side, and transposed convolutions are used at each decoder stage for upsampling and to match the output dimension with the input. The final segmentation map is generated using a $1 \times 1 \times 1$ convolutional filter followed by softmax activation.

2.2   Misclassification Loss

This section explains how we formulated the proposed misclassification loss (MC loss); we also provide Fig. 3 to illustrate the flow of different operations involved. The initial segmentation mask (S_{DCE}) is obtained from the logits (L_{gts}) of the trained nnUNet using softmax, followed by a round operation as follows:

$$S_{DCE} = \lfloor SoftMax(L_{gts}) \rceil \tag{2}$$

where $\lfloor \rceil$ represents the round operation. As the derivative for the round operation is not defined, we utilize a straight-through estimator (STE) to enable gradient forwarding through the round operation in the backward pass [2]. In this way, we can utilize the round operation within the chain rule and still be able to backpropagate from the proposed loss function. The ablation study in Sect. 3.1 explains the motivation for using the differentiable way of extracting the segmentation map from the logits.

The initial segmentation S_{DCE} contains the foreground and background segmentation mask. To obtain the misclassified points map (MPM) we only need the foreground segmentation mask denoted by S^*_{DCE}. A differentiable eXclusive OR (XOR) operation is performed between the foreground of the segmentation mask (S^*_{DCE}) and the ground-truth (GT) to obtain the misclassified points map.

$$MPM = S^*_{DCE} \otimes GT = S^*_{DCE} + GT - 2 \times S^*_{DCE} \cdot GT \tag{3}$$

where $\otimes$ represents the XOR operation.

The MPM contains all the voxels where the network was unable to predict the correct label for either foreground or background. This map includes false positives (FPs) and false negatives (FNs); we can further process the MPM and extract each of them as follows.

$$FNs = MPM \cdot GT \tag{4}$$

$$FPs = MPM \cdot (1 - GT) \tag{5}$$

At this stage, we have identified the errors made by the network; based on this, we can generate a new input and target on the fly to focus only on the misclassified logits (MCLs) as below:

$$MCLs = MPM \cdot L_{gts} \tag{6}$$

A cross-entropy loss is computed between misclassified logits (MCLs) and the false negatives (FNs). The FNs already contain the locations of FPs, with their corresponding values as zeros. So, the loss between MCLs and FNs tries to learn all FPs voxels in MCLs as background and all FNS voxels in MCLs as foreground. i.e.

$$L_{CE}(MCLs, FNs) = -(FNs\log(MCLs) + (1 - FNs)\log(1 - MCLs)) \quad (7)$$

Finally, the MC loss is calculated by multiplying $L_{CE}(MCLs, FNs)$ with the number of non-zero voxels in the misclassified points map denoted as α, which is the total number of false positives and false negatives.

$$L_{MC} = L_{CE}(MCLs, FNs) \cdot \alpha \quad (8)$$

3   Experiments

Dataset Description. The dataset is provided by the SEG.A. MICCAI-2023 challenge, which intends to develop automatic AVT segmentation algorithms. The dataset comprises 56 computed tomography angiography (CTA) scans [21]. The scans are collected from three different locations and various hospitals, which include KiTS [7,8], RIDER [1], and Dongyang Hospital. The dataset comes with an in-plane spatial resolution of 512×512 and 512×666 and with varying numbers of Axial slices depending on the location and hospital. The dataset includes both healthy and patients with aortic dissections (AD), and abdominal aortic aneurysms (AAA). A semi-automatic method was used for AVT annotation, where a manual local threshold is first applied followed by an automatic Grow-Cut region growing algorithm [21]. 3D Slicer[2] was used for performing the above steps to acquire AVT segmentation ground truth. A more detailed overview of the dataset is provided in [21].

Training Details. The proposed framework was implemented using PyTorch (1.11.0), and all the experiments were conducted using an NVIDIA A100 GPU with 40 GB RAM [26]. As a pre-processing step, the CTA scans are resampled to a resolution of $1.88 \times 1.88 \times 3.67 \, \text{mm}^3$. Each scan was normalized using z-score normalization. Different data augmentation strategies were utilized: including rotation, shifting, scaling, elastic deformation, Gaussian noise, Gaussian blur, and random bias field. We randomly shuffled the 56 samples and evaluated all models with 5-fold cross-validation in the validation phase, as suggested by the organizers. We also validated the proposed algorithm on the challenge validation set.

---

[2] https://www.slicer.org/.

Table 1. Differentiable vs non-differentiable quantitative results for SEG.A. challenge data using 5-fold cross-validation split. The best results are in **bold**.

Differentiable XOR-Operation	Non-Differentiable XOR-Operation	Differentiable Segmentation Extraction	Non-Differentiable Segmentation Extraction	Training time (Hours)↓	Dice Score↑
✗	✓	✗	✓	75.7	0.927
✗	✓	✓	✗	74.8	0.928
✓	✗	✗	✓	74.9	0.931
✓	✗	✓	✗	**73.6**	**0.934**

3.1 Ablation Studies

We conducted three ablation studies to explore the different techniques contributing to the MC loss function. The experiments for the first ablation study (differentiable vs. non-differentiable components) were performed using 5-fold cross-validation, while the remaining two studies were conducted using only the first fold. For all the tables in the paper, the upward arrow (↑) indicates that higher is better while the downward arrow (↓) shows lower is better.

Differentiable vs. Non-differentiable Components. The proposed MC loss has two important components that can be implemented using either differentiable or non-differentiable techniques. (1) extraction of the segmentation map from predicted logits, and (2) the XOR operation to generate the misclassified points map. The argmax operation is utilized to get the indices of the maximum value from the logits. However, this operation is not differentiable, which limits its use within loss function design. In order to get a differentiable conversion of logits to segmentation, we replace argmax with a chain of operations that convert logits to segmentation in the forward pass and still have gradients for the backward pass. We achieve this by first applying softmax, followed by round operation. As the round operation is also non-differentiable, we utilize a straight-through estimator (STE) for its gradient propagation in the backward pass [2].

Logic gates play an important role in designing efficient neural networks. Conventionally, logic gates are non-differentiable and do not allow training with gradient descent. Inspired by [19] which proposes differentiable logic gate ideas, our MC loss employs a differentiable XOR operation to enable the back-propagation of gradients.

Table 1 showcases the outcome of this ablation study in terms of training time, and Dice score. All the experiments are performed using a single NVIDIA A100 GPU with 40 GB RAM [26]. The training was performed for 1000 epochs, and the training time mentioned is for all five folds. We found that using differentiable components for the MC loss can reduce the training time ∼ 2 h with improved Dice Score. Replacing the argmax operation with our proposed differentiable segmentation extraction method (given by Eq. 2) reduces the training time by ∼ 1 h.

Table 2. Choice of loss function to define the MC Loss between MCLs and FNs.

Loss Function	Dice Score↑
Mean square error	0.914
Dice Loss (MCLs, FNs) with mask = None	0.916
Dice Loss (L_{gts},GT) with mask = MPM	0.920
Cross-Entropy Loss	**0.924**

Choice of Loss Function for MC Loss. After identifying the misclassified logits, we can use a variety of loss functions to define the proposed MC loss. We experimented with four different losses here, mean square error (MSE), Dice loss, and Dice loss by using MPM as a mask and cross-entropy loss. Table 2 lists the quantitative results for the choice of the loss function to implement MC loss using data from the first fold. Empirically, we found that cross-entropy loss outperforms the others for the SEG.A. 2023 challenge dataset. However, we argue that it might depend on the dataset as well, so for different datasets, similar experiments can be repeated in future work.

Choice of the Balancing Factor λ. As given by Eq. 1, the proposed MC loss is trained in combination with L_{DCE}. Also, as indicated by Eq. 8 the MC loss is multiplied by the number of non-zero voxels in the misclassified points map denoted by α, so the scale of the MC Loss and L_{DCE} are not the same. In order to bring them to the same scale we used the balancing factor λ (introduced in Sect. 2). λ also controls the contributions of each term in Eq. 1. We empirically found that using a large λ reduces the overall performance, as the network overly focusses on the misclassified points map, and the True Positives (TPs), identified in the first training stage are affected, as shown in Table 3. We

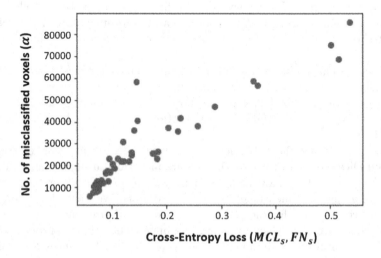

Fig. 4. Variation of cross-entropy loss against the number of non-zero voxels in the misclassified points map α.

Table 3. Ablation study for choosing the balancing factor λ to weight the effect of MC loss and L_{DCE}.

Value of balancing factor λ	Dice Score↑	True Positives↑	False Positives↓	False Negatives↓
0×10^{-5}	0.911	441,108	29,901	55,971
1×10^{-5}	0.918	449,123	26,189	53,359
2×10^{-5}	0.919	448,956	25,780	52,935
5×10^{-5}	**0.924**	**449,978**	**23,150**	50,280
8×10^{-5}	0.922	448989	25,761	**50,140**
1×10^{-4}	0.912	448958	28,254	57,989

can also observe from the table that, using a very low value has no effect on the previously obtained performance. Figure 4 shows how the MC loss varies for network predictions having a different number of misclassified voxels. The graph is plotted for the validation samples of the first fold.

3.2   Results and Discussions

The experimental results are compared with the nnUNet baseline (trained with Dice cross entropy loss and without the proposed loss) and a UNet architecture. The results are evaluated using the Dice score and Hausdorff Distance (HD) [17]. Table 4 lists the quantitative comparison on the random 5-fold cross-validation split. The proposed method outperforms the nnUNet baseline and vanilla UNet both in terms of Dice score and HD. Although the improvement in terms of Dice score and HD is 1%, it highlights the importance of the proposed MC loss to retrieve the overall structure of the AVT, as shown in Fig. 1. It can remove FPs that are not part of the main fine-scale structure and can recover the FNs as well. We found that these types of connections are very important in clinical applications where blood flow is estimated and requires flow distribution analysis in the entire aorta [6,25]. All these tasks require segmenting the Aorta as a preliminary step in order to generate a tetrahedral mesh.

Additional visual results are provided in Fig. 5 showcasing axial, coronal, and sagittal views of a computed tomography angiography (CTA) scan. Different colors are assigned to differentiate between predictions (red), ground truth (green), and overlap of predictions and ground truth (yellow). These correspond to true positives (yellow), false positives (red), and false negative (green) predictions.

The last column of Fig. 5 demonstrates that the proposed MC loss can recover the FNs missed by the first stage training (row-1 and row-3), also it is evident that it can remove the FPs from row-2 of Fig. 5.

4   Limitations

This section presents limitations of the proposed method, including cases where the MC loss does not yield an improvement in segmenting AVT. In some cases,

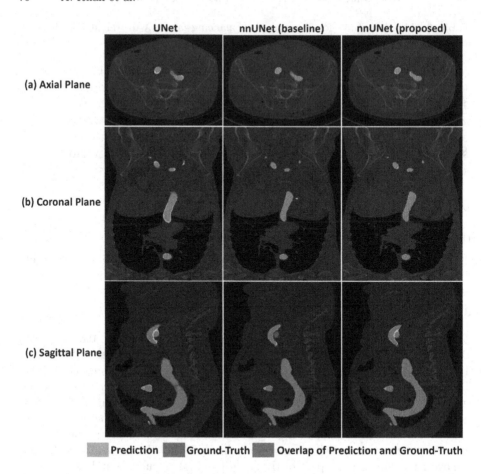

Fig. 5. Qualitative results of AVT segmentation along different views, (a) axial, (b) coronal, and (c) sagittal plane. (Color figure online)

Table 4. Quantitative results for SEG.A. challenge data using 5-fold cross-validation split. The best results are in **bold**.

Segmentation Network	Loss function	Dice Score↑	Hausdorff Distance (mm) ↓
UNet	Dice-cross-Entropy	0.886	7.62
nnUNet	Dice-cross-Entropy	0.921	4.33
nnUNet	Dice-cross-Entropy + MC Loss	**0.934**	**3.55**

the proposed method is unable to fully remove all the FPs, as shown in Fig. 6. Nevertheless, it still results in a partial reduction in FPs (as indicated by the red bounding box in Fig. 6) and contributes to overall improved accuracy, as evident

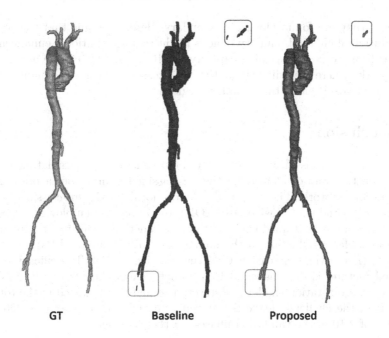

GT   **Baseline**   **Proposed**

Fig. 6. Bad cases where the proposed MC Loss cannot completely remove the FPs (indicated by Red color Bounding Box), and for some voxels, it can help to get rid of all FPs (indicated by Green color Bounding Box). (Color figure online)

by the corresponding Dice Score and HD. We also note that in some regions, it can help to eliminate all FPs (highlighted by the green color box in Fig. 6).

Figure 7 showcases another limitation of the proposed approach, where it is unable to remove the FPs that are connected to the TPs (along the boundary of the segmented regions). In addition, it cannot successfully reduce the FNs

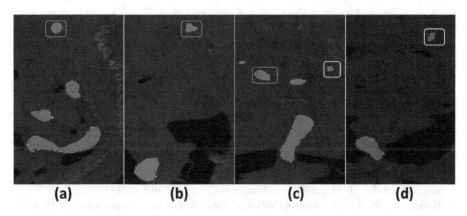

(a)   **(b)**   **(c)**   **(d)**

Fig. 7. Limitations of the proposed method for the cases where misclassified voxels are connected to TPs. A red color bounding box is drawn for FPs, and green color for FNs. (Color figure online)

in cases if they are found along the boundary. Here, we argue that the precise segmentation along the boundary regions might require additional enhancement modules to increase the learning capacity of MC Loss. This can be a potential future work, where we will extend the MC Loss to give more weight to the misclassified voxels along the boundary regions.

5 Conclusion

We propose a misclassification loss (MC loss) function by formulating a simple yet effective way of identifying the misclassified points from a pre-trained segmentation network. The proposed MC loss localizes the misclassified logits using a differentiable eXclusive-OR (XOR) operation. We employ MC loss for fine-tuning a network trained with existing loss functions. This fine-tuning using MC loss enables a reduction in the number of False Positives (FPs) and False Negatives (FNs) while increasing the True Positives (TPs). The efficacy of the proposed method is demonstrated by conducting experiments on the SEG.A. 2023 aorta segmentation challenge dataset. The method is ranked in the top six positions of the challenge leaderboard and achieved a Dice score of 0.926 and HD(mm) of 2.10 in the validation phase-1 of the challenge.

Acknowledgements. This work acknowledges the support of the National Institute for Health Research Barts Biomedical Research Centre (NIHR203330). This research work is also funded by the mini-Centre for Doctoral Training (CDT) award through the Faculty of Science and Engineering, Queen Mary University of London, United Kingdom. The authors also thank mini-CDT partners, including NVIDIA Corporation, Circle Cardiovascular Imaging, and Conavi Medical. The proposed research work utilised Queen Mary's Andrena HPC facility, supported by QMUL Research-IT.

References

1. Zhao, B.: Data From RIDER Lung CT. The Cancer Imaging Archive (2015)
2. Bengio, Y., Léonard, N., Courville, A.: Estimating or propagating gradients through stochastic neurons for conditional computation. arXiv preprint arXiv:1308.3432 (2013)
3. Cao, L., et al.: Fully automatic segmentation of type B aortic dissection from CTA images enabled by deep learning. Eur. J. Radiol. **121**, 108713 (2019)
4. Edelsbrunner, Letscher, Zomorodian: Topological persistence and simplification. Discrete Comput. Geom. **28**, 511–533 (2002)
5. Fantazzini, A., et al.: 3D automatic segmentation of aortic computed tomography angiography combining multi-view 2D convolutional neural networks. Cardiovasc. Eng. Technol. **11**, 576–586 (2020)
6. Garcia, J., et al.: Distribution of blood flow velocity in the normal aorta: effect of age and gender. J. Magn. Reson. Imaging **47**(2), 487–498 (2018)
7. Heller, N., et al.: The kits19 challenge data: 300 kidney tumor cases with clinical context, CT semantic segmentations, and surgical outcomes. arXiv preprint arXiv:1904.00445 (2019)

8. Heller, N., et al.: The state of the art in kidney and kidney tumor segmentation in contrast-enhanced CT imaging: results of the KiTS19 challenge. Med. Image Anal. **67**, 101821 (2021)
9. Hu, X., et al.: Topology-Aware Segmentation Using Discrete Morse Theory. ICLR (2021)
10. Hu, X.: Structure-aware image segmentation with homotopy warping. Adv. Neural. Inf. Process. Syst. **35**, 24046–24059 (2022)
11. Hu, X., Li, F., Samaras, D., Chen, C.: Topology-preserving deep image segmentation. In: Advances in Neural Information Processing Systems, vol. 32 (2019)
12. Isensee, F., et al.: nnU-Net: a self-configuring method for deep learning-based biomedical image segmentation. Nat. Methods **18**(2), 203–211 (2021)
13. Jin, Y., et al.: AI-based aortic vessel tree segmentation for cardiovascular diseases treatment: status quo. arXiv preprint arXiv:2108.02998 (2021)
14. Li, Z., et al.: Lumen segmentation of aortic dissection with cascaded convolutional network. In: Pop, M., et al. (eds.) STACOM 2018. LNCS, vol. 11395, pp. 122–130. Springer, Cham (2019). https://doi.org/10.1007/978-3-030-12029-0_14
15. Members, W.G., et al.: 2010 ACCF/AHA/AATS/ACR/ASA/SCA/SCAI/SIR/ STS/SVM guidelines for the diagnosis and management of patients with thoracic aortic disease: a report of the American college of cardiology foundation/American heart association task force on practice guidelines, American association for thoracic surgery, American college of radiology, American stroke association, society of cardiovascular anesthesiologists, society for cardiovascular angiography and interventions, society of interventional radiology, society of thoracic surgeons, and society for vascular medicine. Circulation **121**(13), e266–e369 (2010)
16. Mosinska, A., Marquez-Neila, P., Koziński, M., Fua, P.: Beyond the pixel-wise loss for topology-aware delineation. In: Proceedings of the IEEE Conference on Computer Vision and Pattern Recognition, pp. 3136–3145 (2018)
17. Müller, D., Soto-Rey, I., Kramer, F.: Towards a guideline for evaluation metrics in medical image segmentation. BMC. Res. Notes **15**(1), 1–8 (2022)
18. Pepe, A., et al.: Detection, segmentation, simulation and visualization of aortic dissections: a review. Med. Image Anal. **65**, 101773 (2020)
19. Petersen, F., Borgelt, C., Kuehne, H., Deussen, O.: Deep differentiable logic gate networks. Adv. Neural. Inf. Process. Syst. **35**, 2006–2018 (2022)
20. PyTorchArgMax, Returns the indices of the maximum values of a tensor across a dimension (2023)
21. Radl, L., et al.: AVT: multicenter aortic vessel tree CTA dataset collection with ground truth segmentation masks. Data Brief **40**, 107801 (2022)
22. Ronneberger, O., Fischer, P., Brox, T.: U-Net: convolutional networks for biomedical image segmentation. In: Navab, N., Hornegger, J., Wells, W.M., Frangi, A.F. (eds.) MICCAI 2015, Part III. LNCS, vol. 9351, pp. 234–241. Springer, Cham (2015). https://doi.org/10.1007/978-3-319-24574-4_28
23. Shit, S., et al.: clDice-a novel topology-preserving loss function for tubular structure segmentation. In: Proceedings of the IEEE/CVF Conference on Computer Vision and Pattern Recognition, pp. 16560–16569 (2021)
24. Simonyan, K., Zisserman, A.: Very deep convolutional networks for large-scale image recognition. ICLR (2015)
25. Sotelo, J., et al.: Fully three-dimensional hemodynamic characterization of altered blood flow in bicuspid aortic valve patients with respect to aortic dilatation: a finite element approach. Front. Cardiovasc. Med. **9**, 885338 (2022)
26. This research utilised Queen Mary's Andrena HPC facility, supported by QMUL Research-IT

Deep Learning-Based Segmentation and Mesh Reconstruction of the Aortic Vessel Tree from CTA Images

Theodoros Panagiotis Vagenas$^{(\boxtimes)}$ (ID), Konstantinos Georgas (ID), and George K. Matsopoulos

Biomedical Engineering Lab (BEL), School of Electrical and Computer Engineering, National Technical University of Athens, 15780 Athens, Greece
{tpvagenas,kostasgeo,gmatsopoulos}@biomed.ntua.gr

Abstract. Segmentation of the Aortic Vessel Tree (AVT) in the Computed Tomography Angiography (CTA) images is pivotal for the diagnosis and monitoring of the aortic diseases. Identifying changes in the AVT structure requires high-quality reconstructions that can enable the accurate comparison of the AVT geometry between follow-up scans. However, manual delineation of the whole AVT is a very time-consuming and labor-intensive procedure that can stall the clinical workflow. In this paper, a Convolutional Neural Network (CNN) methodology is implemented based on the SegResNet architecture for the automatic segmentation of the AVT. A training scheme including preprocessing and data augmentation is designed for the memory-efficient and effective learning of the model parameters. Furthermore, reconstructed surfaces from the initially extracted segmentations are produced through the Marching cubes algorithm and surface correction techniques. The proposed methodology is evaluated in the public SEG.A. grand challenge dataset where in a 5-fold cross-validation experiment it achieved DSC coefficient 91.70%, Recall 91.70%, Precision 91.90% and Hausdorff distance 5.17 mm.

Keywords: Aortic Vessel Tree Segmentation · Computed Tomography Angiography · Deep Learning · Medical Image Analysis

1 Introduction

As the main arterial conduit, the aorta is crucial to the functioning of the human circulatory system because it facilitates the effective transfer of oxygen-rich blood from the heart to numerous peripheral tissues and organs [13]. One cannot exaggerate its anatomical and functional importance, particularly in light of the possible consequences of aortic diseases [18]. If left undiagnosed or untreated, conditions like aortic aneurysms and aortic dissections can result in serious consequences including rupture, internal bleeding, and even unexpected death.

The Aortic Vessel Tree (AVT) may be reconstructed in three dimensions, and computed tomography angiography (CTA) is at the forefront of contemporary

© The Author(s), under exclusive license to Springer Nature Switzerland AG 2024
A. Pepe et al. (Eds.): SEGA 2023, LNCS 14539, pp. 80–94, 2024.
https://doi.org/10.1007/978-3-031-53241-2_7

diagnostic techniques [20]. Visualizing and segmenting the AVT is a prognosis tool as well as a diagnostic procedure. The quantification of illness development, evaluation of treatment measures, and forecasting of possible risk factors for aortic disorders can all be aided by accurate segmentation.

The usual method of outlining the AVT has been manual segmentation, albeit this method has certain drawbacks. In addition to requiring a lot of time, manual segmentation can result in inter-observer variability and is prone to human fatigue. Variable interpretations may result from this discrepancy with possible negative effects on treatment choices and ultimately patient outcomes.

Automated segmentation techniques are a possible replacement that have just emerged. These techniques seek to offer reliable, timely, and precise delineations of the AVT. Although conventional and deep learning-based techniques have been proposed earlier for the automatic segmentation of AVT, it is still difficult to capture the complex AVT structure, in part because various CTA scans have variable picture quality and features. To improve the practical applicability of automated approaches and ensure that they can handle the strict requirements of cardiovascular care, these issues must be resolved. In this paper, a fully automatic segmentation methodology for the AVT based on Convolutional Neural Networks (CNN) is implemented. The methodology includes all the steps of preprocessing, training, surface reconstruction, and segmentation validation for the delineation of AVT. The article's main contributions are summarized below:

- A fast and accurate Deep Learning-based AVT segmentation framework capable of delineating the AVT from CTA images acquired with various parameters from different clinical environments. The proposed methodology is trained with a limited number of samples by exploiting image augmentations and window-based training and inference.
- A mesh construction methodology that first produces the reconstructed surface geometries from the initially extracted segmentation masks and then refines them to create a watertight mesh to be used for modeling the AVT. A high-quality reconstruction is required for the analysis of blood flow and simulations related to endovascular surgery.
- Extensive experiments were conducted for the evaluation of the method on the SEG.A. Grand Challenge dataset. The proposed segmentation scheme outperformed many state-of-the-art methodologies for segmentation. An ablation study of the main components affecting the accuracy is also provided. Both qualitative and quantitative analyses of the resulting segmentation masks and the surface meshing of the AVT are thoroughly conducted and presented.

2   Related Works

Historically, segmentation in medical images relied heavily on conventional methods, which often involved manual or semi-automatic techniques. These methods, while effective, were labor-intensive and prone to variability. Both conventional and deep learning-based methodologies have been proposed for the segmentation of the aorta region. The [4] proposes a combination of a parametric intensity model for the segmentation and an elastic intensity-based method for the registration step in order to segment and quantify the aortic arch. In [22] the segmentation of the coronary artery tree is performed through the enhancement of the vessels and the application of the otsu threshold technique. The feasibility of a detection method for the localization of potential useful landmarks by exploiting intensity-based and geometrical characteristics from CTA is conducted in [24].

Recent developments in medical imaging have ushered in a new era of computational methods intended to improve the efficacy and accuracy of diagnostic procedures. For its ability to automate complex tasks like the segmentation of anatomical features in CT scans, deep learning techniques have attracted a lot of interest. By leveraging large datasets and intricate neural network architectures, deep learning models can learn and generalize complex patterns.

In order to segment the thoracic aorta, abdominal aorta, and iliac arteries, Bozkir et al. [26] used a variety of deep learning architectures, including U-Net, U-Net attention, and Inception U-Netv2. Notably, their analysis showed that the Inception U-Netv2 model performed better at segmentation, significantly reducing the manual effort for doctors.

In the exploration of the 3D aorta segmentation, a study published in NCBI proposed a novel approach that leverages multi-view 2D convolutional networks for a spatially coherent segmentation of various aortic regions [10]. This approach underscores the potential of integrating multiple perspectives to enhance the accuracy of 3D segmentations. Additionally, cascaded convolution networks for the lumen segmentation of the aortic dissection by delineating it in two steps have been proposed in [14], while cascade notion combined with the polar transform was also utilized in [3] for the aorta segmentation. UNet models were applied for the segmentation of aortic dissection with very promising results in [6]. In [13] aorta and its branches are segmented from thorax CT and CTA images through a deep learning technique followed by particle filters.

The effectiveness of deep learning in the totally automated segmentation of abdominal aortic aneurysms from CT images was emphasized in a research published in Frontiers [1]. Another noteworthy research from MDPI explored the potential of 2D convolutional neural networks in segmenting 3D aorta CT images, further emphasizing the transformative capabilities of deep learning techniques in this domain [5]. Deep learning techniques are being studied to assist diagnosis of diseases and the planning of surgical treatments where precise delineation of the aorta and its branches is essential. However, the structure of the aorta with the branch arteries imposes several difficulties that should be further studied. In this work, deep learning methodologies are studied and implemented for the segmentation of AVT from 3D CTA images. The produced segmentations are evaluated both in terms of overlap with the ground truth mask and in terms of distance between the delineated mask and ground truth. The produced segmentation mask is further processed in order to create a reconstructed mesh to be utilized in the clinical workflow. To conclude, not only an AVT segmentation method based on deep learning is proposed but also it is complemented by a suitable mesh reconstruction and evaluated for its clinical usage.

3 Methodology

In this section, the main part of the methodology including the segmentation of the targeted structure and the surface reconstruction will be presented. The preprocessing step, the segmentation method with the neural network, the training scheme and the loss function will be described followed by the mesh creation method.

3.1 Preprocessing

To ensure uniformity and consistency across datasets considering all of the heterogeneity in image acquisition settings, rigorous preprocessing is required. In order to achieve this, a first Intensity Normalization was used, followed by clipping to the Hounsfield units (HU) range of $(-1024, 3071)$, a standard determined from previous research [19]. This action was essential to reducing the impact of potential outliers. Then, in order to ensure the inclusion of typical soft tissue values and the preservation of the intricate details of the aorta region, a refinement step was taken to clip intensities to the range $(-275, 1900)$. After that, it was scaled to the $[0, 1]$ range to assist training.

Data augmentation techniques were used to increase the method's robustness even more. Specifically, Random Flipping, Random Rotating, and Random Shifting Intensity were applied with a probability of 25%. The selection of a 25% probability for the application of data augmentation techniques was the result of an iterative experimental process. This value was determined through a series of tests to balance diversity in the training data and maintain the representativeness of the original dataset. A lower probability failed to introduce sufficient variability, while a higher probability led to augmented data that was too far from the clinical data, potentially introducing artifacts that the model could learn as features. The chosen 25% probability enabled the model to learn from a more diverse set of examples without overfitting to noise, which was evidenced by improved performance metrics on a held-out validation set. Conclusively, after a meticulous analysis of the mean, standard deviation, and median spacing values from the training set, images were resampled to a standardized spacing of $(1.0, 1.0, 1.5)$. The interpolation method was set to bilinear and nearest neighbor for the images and masks respectively.

3.2 Segmentation Method

Neural Network Architecture. The neural network utilized for the segmentation of the Aorta follows the SegResNet [16] architecture based on the implementation from MONAI framework [7] without the use of Variational Autoencoder (VAE). VAE was not utilized in order to reduce GPU memory requirements. The whole architecture consists of a more complex encoder path with more blocks of layers and a lighter decoder path. The encoder path includes three ResNet blocks which downsample the features by 2 in each step by utilizing strided convolutions. More specifically, each ResNet block has group normalization, two convolutions and ReLU activation. ResNet block's architecture is depicted in more detail in Fig. 1. The encoder part is responsible for extracting important features that contain information for the context of the image. Next, there is the bottleneck layer which consists of 4 consecutive ResNet blocks. The main architecture is depicted in Fig. 2. The number of filters in the encoder-bottleneck section was set to be $(8, 16, 32, 64)$ because in this way overfit on the relatively small dataset was prevented and GPU memory requirements of the model were retained relatively low.

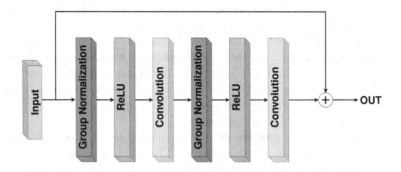

Fig. 1. ResNet block's architecture.

The decoder part aims to extract the required spatial information to achieve the final segmentation. It has a simpler structure which includes one block per layer. In each block, the feature maps from the previous decoder layer are upsampled and then reduced by 2 with the application of a convolution with kernel size of 1. The upsampling in the decoder layers is implemented with transposed convolutions which are trainable modules. The input of each decoder layer is the addition of the related block from the encoder path and the upsampled output of the previous decoder layer. The last layer contains a convolution with 2 filters and a softmax activation for the two classes.

Furthermore, residual connections that improve the network's gradient flow and training dynamics are incorporated into the SegResNet model to make it resilient to changes in imaging conditions and noise. This helps the model perform better on the challenging segmentation task of AVT which presents difficult small arteries.

Training Scheme. During the training procedure due to GPU memory limitations, the initial images were cropped to boxes with size $(96, 96, 96)$ by randomly selecting centers inside or outside the label mask with the same probability. With this configuration, we produced 4 samples per image with a training batch size of 2 boxes. The training parameters of the neural network included: 8 filters

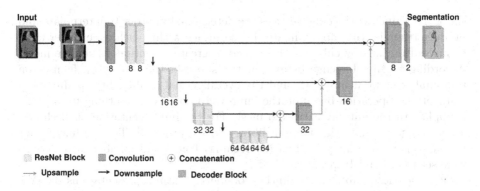

Fig. 2. Neural Network architecture.

in the initial convolution and a dropout probability of 0.35 to prevent overfit. For training an AdamW optimizer with an initial learning rate of 10^{-3} and an exponential learning rate scheduler with $\gamma = 0.9$ were utilized. The training was performed for 600 epochs and the weights with the best DSC (Dice coefficient) in the validation set were saved.

Loss Function. To train the neural network to produce accurate segmentations, the weighted sum of DSC loss and Focal loss (both weights equal to 1) was utilized. DSC metric measures the overlap between the two segmentations while focal loss focuses on the examples that are difficult to be segmented. Below the two metrics are presented for convenience [12]:

$$\mathrm{DSC}_{loss}(y, \hat{y}) = 1 - \frac{2y\hat{y}}{y + \hat{y}} \qquad (1)$$

where y and $\hat{y}$ are the true and predicted segmentations respectively.

$$\mathrm{Focal}_{loss}(p_t) = -\alpha_t (1 - p_t)^\gamma \log(p_t) \qquad (2)$$

where p_t is the output, $\gamma = 2$ and $\alpha \in [0, 1]$. The final loss with $w_1 = w_2 = 1$ was calculated by the following formula:

$$\mathrm{Loss} = w_1 * \mathrm{DSC}_{loss} + w_2 * \mathrm{Focal}_{loss} \qquad (3)$$

3.3   Mesh Construction Method

In this section, the methodology followed for the surface creation of the segmentation result concerning the subtasks of the challenge will be presented. For both visualization and mesh subtasks, the reconstructed surface geometries are produced by applying the Marching Cubes algorithm to the extracted segmentation mask. The marching cubes algorithm [15] is used to generate a surface mesh from volumetric data. A 3D scalar field is divided into small cubes, and the scalar values at the cube vertices are determined in order to interpolate and produce triangles that approximate the isosurface within each cube. After that, triangles from nearby cubes are combined to create a continuous surface mesh. According to the challenge details, in the subtask, the evaluation focuses on the number of branch arteries and the overall visual quality. In this direction, a smoothing operation based on the improved Laplacian smoothing from [9,25] is applied to the initially extracted mesh. For the implementation of mesh creation and smoothing, the Trimesh library was utilized [8]. The parameters for the laplacian smoothing, lambda (smoothing) factor and number of iterations were set to 0.5 and 10 respectively.

For the mesh subtask, the initial volumetric mesh representations of AVT were required to be watertight and in the challenge they were evaluated for their application in the field of computational fluid dynamics using metrics such as the scaled Jacobian. In this regard, the produced mesh before the smoothing operation was corrected by removing singularities, self-intersections, and degenerate elements in order to become watertight. The followed methodology includes steps for the local correction of irregularities in the targeted neighborhoods and it is implemented in pymeshfix library[1] [2]. In its main methodology, the automatic algorithm begins with creating a single combinatorial manifold from the input. Then, it cuts elements with flaws and patches surface holes repetitively until unwanted elements are fixed [2].

4   Experiments and Results

4.1   Dataset

In the present study, we leveraged the comprehensive public dataset sourced from the SEG.A grand challenge [20]. This repository encompasses 56 high-resolution images depicting aortas and their branching components. The KiTS, RIDER, and Dongyang Hospital databases were integrated to create this combined dataset, which provides an in-depth view of the AVT. Every dataset was collected using computed tomography angiography (CTA) images. The ascending aorta, the aortic arch and its branches leading to the head and neck region, as well as the thoracic, abdominal, and lower abdominal aortas, where it further divides into the iliac arteries that extend into the legs, are all clearly visible on the scans. The images have a resolution of 512x(512, 666)x(number of axial slices). Each scan is accompanied by a manually made, semi-automatic ground truth segmentation mask of the aorta vascular tree.

4.2   Evaluation Scheme and Metrics

Our method was implemented with PyTorch and MONAI library [7] and the experiments were conducted in a desktop PC with Nvidia 4090 GPU with 24GB

---

[1] PyMeshFix: https://pymeshfix.pyvista.org/.

GPU memory. For the evaluation of the model, a 5-fold cross-validation technique was applied to the dataset. Four main metrics were used for the evaluation of the produced segmentations. For the first three metrics, their mean value is presented in the tables. The Sørensen-Dice coefficient is widely used for the evaluation of the performance of image segmentation algorithms. It quantifies the similarity/overlap between two sets, the ground truth segmentation, and the segmentation produced by the algorithm. The Dice is calculated by:

$$\text{Dice Coefficient (DSC)} = \frac{2 \cdot |A \cap B|}{|A| + |B|} \tag{4}$$

where A, and B represent the set of voxels in the two segmentations, $|A|,|B|$ represents the total number of voxels in A, B respectively.

Recall is the ratio of true positives (correctly identified positive voxels) to the total number of actual positives.

$$\text{Recall/Sensitivity} = \frac{TP}{TP + FN} \tag{5}$$

Precision is the ratio of true positives to the total number of voxels identified as positive.

$$\text{Precision} = \frac{TP}{TP + FP} \tag{6}$$

where TP, FP and FN represent the number of true positives, false positives and false negatives respectively [23].

Hausdorff distance (HD) is defined by:

$$H(A, B) = \max\{h(A, B), h(B, A)\} \tag{7}$$

$$h(A, B) = \max_{a \in A} \min_{b \in B} \|a - b\| \tag{8}$$

where H is the directed Hausdorff distance from set A to set B. For the evaluation, the HD 95th percentile was calculated, and the median value from the samples is presented in the tables in order to comply with the grand challenge's evaluation values and avoid excessive outliers' influence.

4.3   Ablation Study

In this subsection, we present an ablation study to investigate the impact of various parameters on the segmentation and select the most suitable ones for our target. To save time in experiments, the network was trained for 300 epochs, which was the point at which the loss values began to stabilize. For each experiment, only the studied parameter was altered, with all others held constant, in order to measure its effect on the results.

Effect of the Loss Function. Three loss functions were studied for the segmentation of AVT. It was observed that the combination of a DSC loss and a focal loss yielded superior performance metrics, as presented in Table 1. The use of DSC loss alone did not enable the model to be effectively trained probably due to the difficult structure of the AVT which includes small branches. While the addition of cross-entropy to DSC loss improved the results, it was less effective than focal loss. The addition of focal loss achieved the best results due to its design which focuses on the most challenging regions.

Table 1. Loss functions comparisons.

Loss	DSC	Recall	Precision
DSC	62.37%	55.50%	72.90%
DSC + Cross entropy	81.94%	81.20%	83.00%
DSC + Focal loss	**85.21%**	**83.65%**	**83.65%**

Effect of the Upsampling Method in the Decoder. The method of upsampling in the decoder path demonstrated a significant influence on the reconstruction and the final segmentation mask. Table 2 shows the segmentation results of the two compared methods, the linear interpolation, and the transpose convolution. Transposed convolution, despite increasing the model's complexity, enhanced the segmentation performance by approximately 8% in terms of DSC, representing a substantial improvement.

Table 2. Upsampling techniques comparisons.

Method	DSC	Recall	Precision
Linear interpolation	77.20%	72.65%	83.00%
Transpose convolutions	**85.21%**	**83.65%**	**83.65%**

Effect of the optimizer. Finally, the choice of optimizer was assessed by testing three of the most commonly used options. The AdamW which is a more recent version of Adam including an improved weight decay achieved the best results in the experiments, as shown in Table 3. The experimental results underscore the importance of selecting an appropriate optimizer to enhance model training and performance.

4.4   Learning Curves

In Fig. 3 the loss values and the DSC metric are plotted for both the training and the validation set. We can point out that the loss function is decreasing during

Table 3. Comparison results for the optimizers.

Optimizer	DSC	Recall	Precision
SGD	75.60%	80.21%	73.54%
Adam	79.44%	75.79%	**83.90%**
AdamW	**85.21%**	**83.65%**	83.65%

training for at least 300 epochs where the curve begins stabilizing. Training and validation losses present approximately the same behavior indicating that overfitting during training is avoided. The curve of the DSC metric increases to the value of 90% approximately which is also supported by the final results.

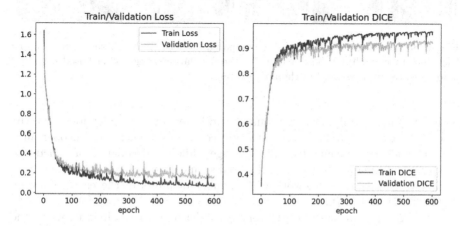

Fig. 3. Training and validation loss and DSC metric curves.

4.5   Qualitative Results

In this subsection qualitative comparison results of the deep learning-based segmentation methodologies are presented. Figure 4 shows three comparative segmentation results produced from the tested methods for examples from the three subdatasets. In the first row, undersegmentation is observed in the UNet mask while SegResNet shows the smoothest AVT mask. In the second and third rows, SegResNet captures most of the small regions from the mask that were missed by the UNet and UNETR. Overall, visualization of the examples supports the ability of the proposed network to capture small regions and avoid false positives.

4.6   Quantitative Results

Following comparison results of tested models in the 5-fold cross-validation in the provided set are presented. During our experiments, the proposed SegResNet-based architecture was compared with some of the most common and representative segmentation networks with the same training schemes.

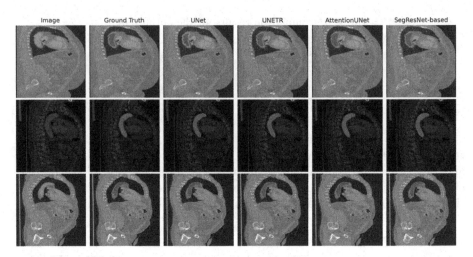

Fig. 4. Segmentation results from the compared models. Each row shows an example from the three small datasets included in the full dataset. SegResNet-based proposed model results are presented in the final column.

- UNet [21]: a Fully Convolutional Neural Network (FCNN) following the encoder-decoder architecture with skip connections where the encoder aims at extracting the context from the image while the decoder reconstructs the spatial information to produce the final segmentation. UNet implementation follows the monai framework with number of filters in the encoder layers: $(16, 32, 64, 128, 256)$.
- UNETR [11]: which also consists of an encoder-decoder architecture where the encoder path includes transformer blocks instead of convolutions in order to capture global spatial dependencies. Training and architectural parameters: feature size: 8, dimension of hidden layer: 768, dimension of feedforward layer: 2048 and number of attention heads: 16.
- AttentionUNet [17]: a UNet-like structure complemented with attention gates which enables the network to remove undesired false positive structures and focus only on the targeted structures. The number of filters per layer in the encoder path was selected as $(16, 32, 64, 128, 256)$. The kernel size was set to 3 and the dropout rate to 0.1.

Experimental results are presented in the Table 4. As it can be observed, the SegResNet achieved the best DSC value of 91.7% where UNet achieved 88.34%, UNETR 88.25%, and AttentionUNet 89.55%. Results show that even though, UNETR and AttentionUNet achieved similar values with SegResNet in recall and precision respectively, SegResNet outperformed them in all metrics concurrently. In addition, the HD metric was very important for this specific task because achieving a small distance between segmentations is required for modeling the aorta and its branches. In this metric SegResNet achieved by large difference the best results among the compared models, with AttentionUNet coming second with 7.44 mm. In this regard, the small HD value of the SegResNet supports its ability to segment the AVT by including small branches of arteries which cannot be quantified by the mean DSC coefficient. Although small branches are the most difficult part to segment, the proposed model presented the best results among the compared ones for this task. To conclude, SegResNet-based architecture achieved the best values in all metrics outperforming the other networks by resulting in both higher sensitivity and fewer false positives.

Table 4. Segmentation results.

Model (means)	DSC	Recall	Precision	HD (mm)
UNet	88.30%	89.70%	87.70%	42.43
UNETR	88.20%	91.20%	85.90%	10.49
AttentionUNet	89.50%	87.90%	91.50%	7.44
SegResNet	**91.70%**	**91.70%**	**91.90%**	**5.17**

4.7   Interpretation in Mesh Quality and Plots

In Fig. 5, an example of the meshes produced by applying the proposed method to the segmentation outputs of the compared models is presented. The first mesh refers to the ground truth and the final to the proposed model. UNet and AttentionUnet failed to delineate a large part of the main segmentation mask and UNETR did not capture the shape of the top part of the aorta. However, the proposed method correctly segmented the largest part of the targeted structure presenting the best AVT mask. It only failed to identify some of the thinner structures which is one of the difficulties of this dataset. The most important observation to be made here is that the figure also indicates high quality in the watertight meshes resulting from the combination of the Marching cubes algorithm and the additional mesh method with the local corrections. High-quality meshes were a target of this method because they are required in order to be utilized for various tasks of modeling for diagnostic purposes. The high quality of meshes was also supported by the results of the proposed methodology during the corresponding grand challenge subtask "Volumetric meshing of the Aortic Vessel Tree" where our team (BIOMED) won first place.

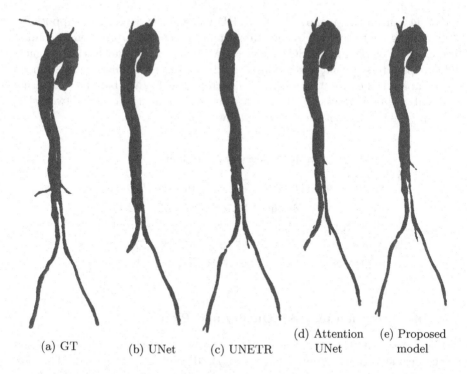

(a) GT   (b) UNet   (c) UNETR   (d) Attention   (e) Proposed
                                                        UNet   model

Fig. 5. Meshes produced by the ground truth and the segmentation models

5   Conclusion

Segmentation and modeling of the Aortic Vessel Tree is crucial for the diagnosis and monitoring of patients suffering from aortic diseases. However, manual delineation of the AVT from 3D images requires a great amount of time which can be infeasible for the real clinical workflow. In this article, a SegResNet-based methodology is designed and implemented for the automatic and accurate segmentation of the AVT from CTA images. The segmentation method was complemented with the construction and refinement of the reconstructed surfaces which are required for the modeling of AVT in procedures such as identifying alterations in follow-up scans and producing accurate simulations. The proposed scheme was evaluated on the SEG.A. Grand Challenge, where results indicate high accuracy in the segmentation and modeling of AVT.

References

1. Abdolmanafi, A., Forneris, A., Moore, R.D., Martino, E.S.D.: Deep-learning method for fully automatic segmentation of the abdominal aortic aneurysm from computed tomography imaging. Front. Cardiovasc. Med. **9**, 1040053 (2023). https://doi.org/10.3389/FCVM.2022.1040053
2. Attene, M.: A lightweight approach to repairing digitized polygon meshes. Vis. Comput. **26**, 1393–1406 (2010). https://doi.org/10.1007/S00371-010-0416-3
3. Bencevic, M., Habijan, M., Galic, I., Babin, D.: Using the polar transform for efficient deep learning-based aorta segmentation in CTA images. Proc. Elmar - Int. Symp. Electron. Mar. 191–194 (2022). https://doi.org/10.1109/ELMAR55880.2022.9899786
4. Biesdorf, A., et al.: Segmentation and quantification of the aortic arch using joint 3d model-based segmentation and elastic image registration. Med. Image Anal. **16**, 1187–1201 (2012). https://doi.org/10.1016/J.MEDIA.2012.05.010
5. Bonechi, S., et al.: Segmentation of aorta 3d CT images based on 2d convolutional neural networks. Electronics **10**(20), 2559 (2021). https://doi.org/10.3390/ELECTRONICS10202559
6. Cao, L., et al.: Fully automatic segmentation of type b aortic dissection from CTA images enabled by deep learning. Eur. J. Radiol. **121**, 108713 (2019). https://doi.org/10.1016/J.EJRAD.2019.108713
7. Cardoso, M.J., et al.: MONAI: an open-source framework for deep learning in healthcare, November 2022. https://arxiv.org/abs/2211.02701v1
8. Dawson-Haggerty et al.: trimesh https://trimsh.org/
9. Desbrun, M., Meyer, M., Schröder, P., Barr, A.H.: Implicit fairing of irregular meshes using diffusion and curvature flow. In: Proceedings of the 26th Annual Conference on Computer Graphics and Interactive Techniques, SIGGRAPH 1999, pp. 317–324, July 1999. https://doi.org/10.1145/311535.311576
10. Fantazzini, A., et al.: 3d automatic segmentation of aortic computed tomography angiography combining multi-view 2d convolutional neural networks. Cardiovasc. Eng. Technol. **11**, 576 (2020). https://doi.org/10.1007/S13239-020-00481-Z
11. Hatamizadeh, A., et al.: UNETR: transformers for 3d medical image segmentation. In: Proceedings - 2022 IEEE/CVF Winter Conference on Applications of Computer Vision, WACV 2022, pp. 1748–1758 (2022). https://doi.org/10.1109/WACV51458.2022.00181
12. Jadon, S.: A survey of loss functions for semantic segmentation. In: 2020 IEEE Conference on Computational Intelligence in Bioinformatics and Computational Biology, CIBCB 2020, October 2020. https://doi.org/10.1109/CIBCB48159.2020.9277638
13. Jin, Y., Pepe, A., Li, J., Gsaxner, C., Egger, J.: Deep learning and particle filter-based aortic dissection vessel tree segmentation **11600**, 460–465 (2021) https://doi.org/10.1117/12.2588220
14. Li, Z., et al.: Lumen segmentation of aortic dissection with cascaded convolutional network. In: Pop, M., et al. (eds.) STACOM 2018. LNCS, vol. 11395, pp. 122–130. Springer, Cham (2019). https://doi.org/10.1007/978-3-030-12029-0_14
15. Lorensen, W.E., Cline, H.E.: Marching cubes: a high resolution 3d surface construction algorithm. ACM SIGGRAPH Comput. Graph. **21**, 163–169 (1987). https://doi.org/10.1145/37402.37422

16. Myronenko, A.: 3D MRI brain tumor segmentation using autoencoder regular-ization. In: Crimi, A., Bakas, S., Kuijf, H., Keyvan, F., Reyes, M., van Walsum, T. (eds.) BrainLes 2018. LNCS, vol. 11384, pp. 311–320. Springer, Cham (2019). https://doi.org/10.1007/978-3-030-11726-9_28

17. Oktay, O., et al.: Attention u-net: Learning where to look for the pancreas, April 2018. https://arxiv.org/abs/1804.03999v3

18. Pepe, A., et al.: Detection, segmentation, simulation and visualization of aortic dissections: a review. Med. Image Anal. **65**, 101773 (2020). https://doi.org/10.1016/J.MEDIA.2020.101773

19. Peyrin, F., Engelke, K.: CT Imaging: basics and new trends. In: Grupen, C., Buvat, I. (eds.) Handbook of Particle Detection and Imaging, pp. 883–915. Springer, Berlin (2012). https://doi.org/10.1007/978-3-642-13271-1_36

20. Radl, L., et al.: AVT: multicenter aortic vessel tree CTA dataset collection with ground truth segmentation masks. Data Brief **40**, 107801 (2022). https://doi.org/10.1016/J.DIB.2022.107801

21. Ronneberger, O., Fischer, P., Brox, T.: U-Net: convolutional networks for biomed-ical image segmentation. In: Navab, N., Hornegger, J., Wells, W.M., Frangi, A.F. (eds.) MICCAI 2015. LNCS, vol. 9351, pp. 234–241. Springer, Cham (2015). https://doi.org/10.1007/978-3-319-24574-4_28

22. Shams, M., Salem, M.A., Hamad, S., Shedeed, H.A.: Coronary artery tree seg-mentation in computed tomography angiography using otsu method. In: 2017 IEEE 8th International Conference on Intelligent Computing and Information Sys-tems, ICICIS 2017, 2018-January, pp. 416–420, July 2017. https://doi.org/10.1109/INTELCIS.2017.8260081

23. Taha, A.A., Hanbury, A.: Metrics for evaluating 3d medical image segmentation: analysis, selection, and tool. BMC Med. Imaging **15**, 1–28 (2015). https://doi.org/10.1186/S12880-015-0068-X

24. Tahoces, P.G., et al.: Automatic detection of anatomical landmarks of the aorta in CTA images. Med. Biol. Eng. Comput. **58**, 903–919 (2020). https://doi.org/10.1007/S11517-019-02110-X

25. Vollmer, J., Mencl, R., Uller, H.M., Dieser, Z.: Improved laplacian smoothing of noisy surface meshes improved laplacian smoothing of noisy surface meshes (1999)

26. Bozkir, Ö.F., Budak, A., Karatas, H., Ceylan, M.: Segmentation of the aorta in CTA images using deep learning methods, February 2023. https://doi.org/10.21203/RS.3.RS-2559681/V1

RASNet: U-Net-Based Robust Aortic Segmentation Network for Multicenter Datasets

Jihan Zhang[1]([⊠])(iD), Zhen Zhang[2](iD), and Liqin Huang[2](iD)

[1] College of Computer and Data Science, Fuzhou University, Fuzhou 350108, Fujian, China
ericamontblanc@icloud.com, 102104212@fzu.edu.cn
[2] Intelligent Image Processing and Analysis Laboratory, Fuzhou University, Fuzhou 350108, Fujian, China

Abstract. The segmentation and reconstruction of the aortic vessel tree (AVT) is necessary in detecting aortic diseases. Currently, the mainstream method must be deployed manually, which is time-consuming and requires an experienced radiologist/physician. Automatic segmentation methods developed in recent years have performed well on single-centered datasets. However, their performance degraded on multi-centered datasets due to the various specifications of the data. We propose a 3D U-Net-based robust aortic segmentation framework to address the problem. We implied Hounsfield Units (HU) adaptive method during preprocessing to reduce the variety of intensity distribution of the inter-center images. We insert convolutional block attention modules (CBAM) in our network to improve its channel and spatial representation ability. Furthermore, we set a two-stage training process and introduce the Hausdorff distance (HD) loss in the second stage to optimize the structure of the segmentation results. Using a specific validation set collected from the multicenter AVT dataset which includes samples D5, D6, K4, K5, R5, R6, our proposed method reached an average Dice Similarity Coefficient (DSC) of 0.9396 and an average HD of 16.1.

Keywords: Multicenter dataset · Aortic segmentation · 3D U-Net

1 Introduction

The aortic vessel tree (AVT) comprises the aorta and branch arteries and plays a vital part in the circulatory system. Chronic aortic diseases like hypertension change the anatomical features of AVT, cause lesions like aortic dissection or abdominal aortic aneurysms, harm the circulatory system, and even result in aortoclasia with fatal consequences. Therefore, quantitative evaluation of the anatomical features of the AVT helps diagnose aortic diseases and push forward treatments in clinical practice.

Computed tomography angiography (CTA) provides a detailed image of the AVT, allowing the detection of the aorta, branches, and tissues [1]. Currently, the segmentation and reconstruction of the AVT from CTA are deployed manually, which could be subjective and time-consuming. It requires slice-by-slice contouring and takes a long time to create a segmentation mask of the AVT. Moreover, only professional radiologists or physicians can handle these scans and obtain reliable results [2,5]. These disadvantages limit manually reconstructing AVT in clinical practice.

Many automatic AVT segmentation algorithms have been developed and experimented in recent years. Some of these automatic methods are based on deep learning, for example, a 2D-U-Net-based method that achieves a Dice coefficient similarity of 91.20% in the segmentation of aorta and coronary arteries [4]. Other methods rely on graph execution algorithms, for instance, a method based on graph cut attains an average dice metric exceeding 0.9690 in a challenging task of abdominal aorta segmentation in 3D CT images [3]. A few algorithms performed well on abundant single-center aorta CT files. However, different medical centers propose different scanning protocols [1], causing the variety in Hounsfield Unit (HU) values, resolution, vessel tree volume and some other features in multicenter AVT datasets. This difference makes models trained with multicenter datasets perform worse than those trained with single-center datasets in Dice score and Hausdorff distance (HD) [5]. In conclusion, the various feature distribution inter-center is challenging in using deep-learning-based methods in clinical practice.

To address the challenges mentioned above, in this paper, we propose the RASNet, a robust aortic segmentation framework based on 3D U-Net. In order to prohibit the negative impact of multicenter data, it includes a preprocess to limit the variety of HU value range and histogram distribution of inter-center images. We propose a two-stage training process to improve the network's information extraction of the structure of the ground truth mask. We use Dice loss as the only loss function in the first stage. We introduce the HD loss based on weighted HD as a penalty in the second stage to adjust the network and prohibit erroneous predictions with false positives or false negatives. In the network, each sampling block has a convolutional block attention module (CBAM) to allow better focus on prominent parts of CT files and skip the irrelevant background parts. Therefore, the network's recognition of regions with the AVT is improved.

2 Methodology

The overview of our workflow is provided in Fig. 1. A preprocess including threshold truncation, standardization, normalization and block dividing is deployed. The detailed process and results of the method are introduced in Sect. 3.3. After dividing, the input files are converted into limited-sized blocks and fed into the 3D U-Net-CBAM network.

A two-stage training process is designed for the model adjustment. To optimize the model trained with Dice loss in stage one, avoid excrescent or missing of the segmentation masks and make the surface of segmentation results smoother, we introduce the weighted HD loss in stage two.

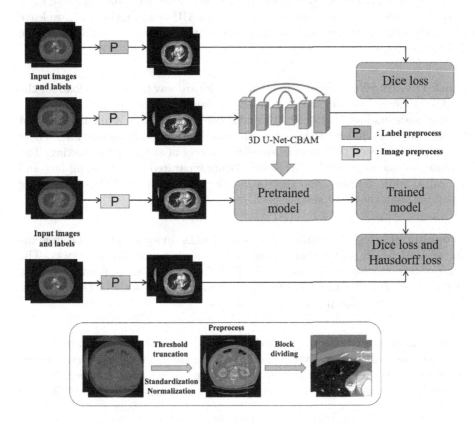

Fig. 1. The workflow of our method and details of preprocess. The input images are preprocessed and fed into the network. The first stage of training provides the Pretrained model trained with Dice loss, and then the model becomes the Trained model in the second stage with the loss function consists of Dice loss and Hausdorff loss.

2.1 Preprocessing

In the preprocessing, the order of the operations is threshold truncation, standardization, normalization and block dividing. The changes in the images through the preprocessing are also exhibited in Fig. 1.

Threshold Truncation. Our observation on the CT files and experiments on training models from truncated training sets have shown that the contrast between the aorta and other tissues seems obvious when the HU range includes [0,500]. Also, we set the window width as 1500 in order to contain all histograms of each CT files. Therefore our strategy of threshold truncation is first get the minimum HU of original data and judge whether it was smaller than -1000. If the minimum is below -1000, we set [0,1500] as the HU range because most of the histograms are distributed in the positive HU range. Otherwise, we leave the minimum unchanged and set the sum of the minimum and 1500 as the maximum HU.

Block Dividing Strategy. The input CT files are way too large to load for the 3D U-Net, so we use the sliding window method to divide the files into blocks with a consistent size of [128,128,32] and stride of [64,64,16]. While training and testing, only one block in the set is processed in the model each time. There is a slight difference between the dividing process of training and testing. The training blocks are saved in drives after being separated from training files and are called while training, and the testing blocks are saved in RAM after being separated from the input testing data.

Cropping Strategy. For training sets, the blocks divided from the original file are selected based on the sum of the binary mask figure in each blocks: The binary figure represents the mask of AVT. If the sum is 0, there is no valid mask in the block, and the block is abandoned to reduce the scale of training sets. Therefore, the training process costs less time.

Standardization Method. To further mitigate the discrepancies in histogram distributions and window level variations among inter-central samples, we map the window levels of all samples to [0,1]. In experiment results in Sect. 3.3, we prove that standardization and normalization can simply reduce the difference in HU.

2.2   Network

Figure 2 exhibits the architecture of our 3D U-Net-CBAM network, which is a combination of the 3D U-Net network and CBAM [8]. The input of our network first goes into one 3D convolution layer, three double 3D convolution layers and three max 3D pooling layers as the downward sampling module. The double 3D convolution layer includes two 3D convolution layers, two batch normalization layers and two ReLU. Then, it passes through a middle 3D convolution layer and the upward sampling module including three transpose convolution layers, three upward double 3D convolution layers and one 3D convolution layer to become the output.

In all downward layers and upward layers, we add CBAM. In downward layers, the module strengthens the network's channel-wise and spacial-wise attention to input data. Also, CBAM can work as the skip connection. The module improves the discrimination of the extracted features and details in upward layers.

According to the comparison between CBAM and other attention modules, for example, the spatial and channel attention block (CSAM) [5], CBAM could be inserted into the layers of U-Net network architecture and improves the performance without putting too much pressure on computing [8].

2.3 Loss Function

Our loss function for the second training stage consists of Dice loss and HD loss with weight, and the percentage is α and $1 - \alpha$. The constant weight α is set to balance the two losses, and we set it to 0.05.

In segmentation and reconstruction, HD reflects the similarity of surface and shape between the ground truth and the prediction. Therefore, it can be introduced as a penalty to prohibit the false positives and false negatives in the predictions.

$$Loss = \alpha * L_{hd}(G, P) + (1 - \alpha) * L_{dice}(G, P) \tag{1}$$

In the loss formula and all formulae below, G is the ground truth and P is the prediction. For loss functions, L_{hd} means the HD loss [7], and L_{dice} means the Dice loss [9].

$$L_{dice} = 1 - Dice(G, P) \tag{2}$$

where

$$Dice(G, P) = \frac{2(|G \cap P|)}{|G| + |P|} \tag{3}$$

The Dice Similarity Coefficient (DSC) is also calculated through formula (3).

$$L_{hd}(G, P) = k * \max \{H(G, P), H(P, G)\} \tag{4}$$

where

$$H(G, P) = \max_{g \in G} \{\min_{p \in P} \{\|g - p\|\}\} \tag{5}$$

In the HD loss function, k represents the weight and we set it 0.01 here. The maximum of the two unidirectional HDs is the HD between ground truth and prediction.

2.4 Postprocess

Rim Truncation. For each testing image, there is a 3D zero array with the same shape as it, and for each block, the output is added to the array according to the block's location in the test image. Since the aorta is always in the center of the image, we set a range according to the x and y coordinates of the image in order to filter the blocks which are distant from the center. Using this filter, we speed up the testing process and remove the unwanted non-central parts of the mask.

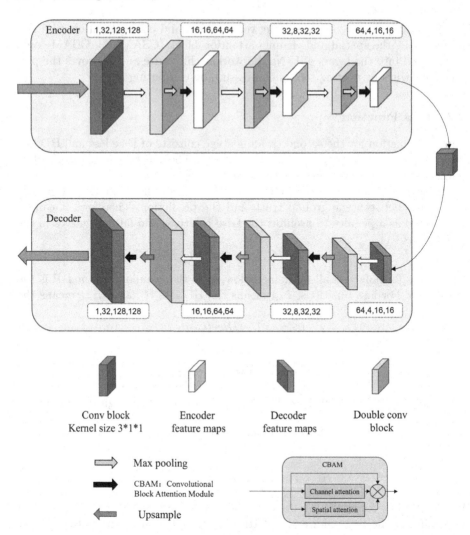

Fig. 2. Our 3D U-Net-CBAM network. 3D U-Net-CBAM is based on 3D U-Net with CBAM in all downward and upward layers.

Retaining the Max Connected Domain. The prediction result may include redundant masks that don't connect to the accurate mask of the aorta. Each part of mask consists a connected domain. After processing rim truncation, the larger domains than the aorta domain are removed since they are away from the center, therefore, there are only the aorta domain and smaller unwanted domains left. By retaining the largest connected domain, the redundant domains are simply removed.

3   Experiments

3.1   The Dataset and Evaluation Method

Dataset. The dataset provided by SEG.A. 2023 Segmentation of the Aorta [10] includes 56 CTA scans of the aortas, their branches and the abdominal areas with iliac arteries. The providers also include semi-automatic segmentation masks as the ground truth [1]. The dataset includes three collections that are taken from the KiTS19 Grand Challenge [11], the RIDER Lung CT dataset [12] and Dongyang Hospital.

As a multicenter dataset, the CT scans from the same center have similar HU value distribution, the same window width, resolution, axial slices and further features. However, the features vary between inter-central images.

All cases in the collections KiTS and Dongyang are healthy, while one case with abdominal aortic aneurysms and five cases with aortic dissection are observed in the RIDER collection. The pathological cases have different structures compared with healthy cases, causing instability in model's performance.

Evaluation Method. The evaluation method includes two accuracy methods: the Dice Similarity Coefficient (DSC) and the Hausdorff Distance (HD).

3.2   Implementation Details

Environmental Settings. We executed the training and inference process based on the environment shown in Table 1.

Training Protocols. In the training process, we use Adam optimizer and a constant learning rate of 0.0001. The training protocols for the two stages are shown in Table 2. To optimize the training time, we set up a one-stage process, directly implying stage two as the only training stage and observing whether this one-stage process can train a model that performs high DSC, low HD within a shorter time than the two-stage process. In the training of 3D U-Net, a larger batch size has a significant enhance on the segmentation performance [6]. Hence, we set a batch size of 20 in order to use a larger amount of samples to update the gradient.

During the experiments, we discovered that in the prediction process, if the patch size is $32 \times 128 \times 128$, the average process time for each sample is 50.18 s. If we set the patch size as $16 \times 64 \times 64$, the average time declines to 16.78 s, and the smaller patch size needs less CPU memory. Nevertheless, the quality of the prediction results made with a $16 \times 64 \times 64$ patch size is usually worse, therefore the choice of patch size is $32 \times 128 \times 128$.

Validation Set Choice. We chose two groups of samples and used them as two validation sets. The validation set 1 includes D5, D6, K4, K5, R5, R6, and the validation set 2 includes D1, D3, K1, K3, R1, R3. Samples in set 2 are the same as the validation sample in another work [5]. We also set two training sets, consisting of the samples apart from the validation sets.

Table 1. Environments and requirements.

System version	Ubuntu 20.04.4 LTS
CPU	12th Gen Intel®Core™i9-12900K × 24
RAM	62.6 GB
GPU	1 NVIDIA Tesla P40 (24G)
CUDA version	11.4
Programming language	Python 3.9
Deep learning framework	Pytorch (Torch 1.11.0, torchvision 0.8.2)
Specific dependencies	scipy

Table 2. Training protocols for stage one and stage two.

Training stages	Stage One	Stage Two
Network initialization	Random weight parameters	Model trained in stage one
Batch size	20	20
Patch size	$32 \times 128 \times 128$	$32 \times 128 \times 128$
Epochs	40	50
Optimizer	Adam	Adam
Learning rate	0.0001	0.0001
Training time	13 h	16.25 h
Loss function	Dice loss	Dice loss and HD loss
Number of workers	16	16

3.3 The HU Features Before and After Preprocess

The HU histograms of raw images R5 and D5 in Fig. 3 indicate that images from different dataset collections significantly differ in the HU distribution and window width. This difference is the main challenge to train one single network with all images from the dataset. Firstly, the threshold truncation changes the maximum and minimum of the image intensity. The image intensity with thick histograms is distributed in regions with a window width of 1500: therefore, the threshold truncation separate the regions from the original regions. Secondly, the standardization and normalization process changed the threshold value into the range [0,1]. The HU histogram of processed images R5 and D5 are in Fig. 4.

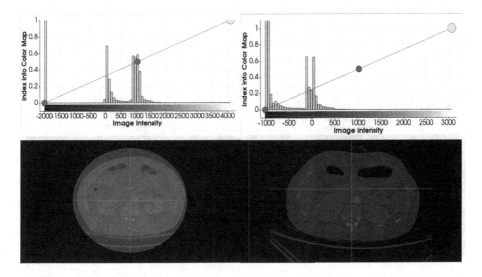

Fig. 3. HU histograms and images of raw sample R5 (left) and D5 (right).

They have the same window width of [0,1], and their HU histogram distributions are similar. The preprocess method is feasible in reducing the difference in HU histograms distribution of images from different centers.

4 Experiment Results

On the validation set 1, we perform ablation experiments to compare the model performance with and without the CBAM, the HD loss and the normalization process. On the validation set 2, we compare the model with another U-Net-based method [5], which is informally mentioned as U-Net-CSAM. In this paper, the performances of proposed methods are evaluated between the prediction of the selected validation sets and the ground truth.

4.1 Results on Validation Set 1

Quantitative Results on Validation Set 1. The performances of models trained with different combinations of processes are shown in Table 3. When using only the baseline network and the necessary measures, i.e., standardization and threshold truncation, the best model reaches an average DSC of 0.9123 and an average HD of 36.3. When using the RASNet, which includes all the measures above, the average DSC becomes 0.9396, and the average HD drops to 16.1. The performances of models trained by the one-stage process are also in Table 3. After using the HD loss, the segmentation results have better branches, and the predictions of samples with aortic dissection present a more detailed mask on the ascending aorta. The model performs better in healthy samples but weaker

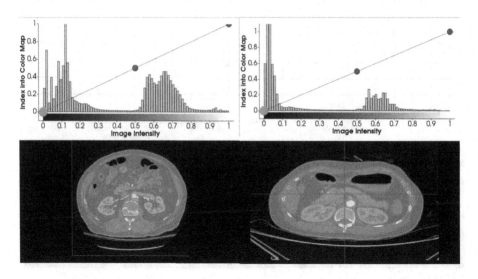

Fig. 4. HU histograms and images of processed sample R5 (left) and D5 (right). Compared with Fig. 3, the region of the aorta in the center of the image is brighter.

in samples with aortic dissection. We also tried different weight on HD loss (α) in training, and the result is that a smaller weight leads the network to smaller DSC than a larger weight, while the HD is only slightly higher.

Table 3. Average DSC and HD on validation set 1.

Method	DSC	HD
baseline	0.9123	36.3
CBAM	0.9232	30.6
CBAM+HD loss, one stage	0.9289	29.4
CBAM+HD loss, two stages, $\alpha = 0.05$	0.9342	24.0
CBAM+HD loss, two stages, $\alpha = 0.4$	0.9262	17.5
CBAM+HD loss, two stages, $\alpha = 0.15$	0.9284	24.7
CBAM+Norm	0.9359	32.1
CBAM+HD loss+Norm, one stage	0.9380	17.6
CBAM+HD loss+Norm, two stages, $\alpha = 0.05$ (RASNet)	0.9396	16.1

Qualitative Results on Validation Set 1. The 2D slices of visualized segmentation results of samples D5, K4, R5 and R6 are presented in Fig. 5, and the 3D reconstruction models of visualized results are shown in Fig. 6.

All the methods make better segmentation results on healthy samples collected from Dongyang Hospital and KiTS and the sample R6 with abdominal aortic aneurysms. On the sample R5, all the methods can't make a complete segmentation on the ascending aorta and the abdominal aorta. However, with a more detailed reconstruction of the connection between the ascending aorta and the heart, some methods' segmentation results of R5 are better than the other methods'.

Figure 7 compares the segmentation details obtained by the one-stage-trained model and those by the two-stage-trained model. The performance of the one-stage process partially avoids false negatives in the mask but includes more false positives close to the iliac artery. The two-stage-trained model does not create false positives in the region. This comparison shows that the two-stage process makes the network learn more information about the structure of the ground truth.

We demonstrate the ablation experiments on the visualized results, which prove that our method is feasible in removing issues caused by different features in multicenter samples. After analyzing the samples with aortic dissection, potential reasons for the inaccurate segmentation result on sample R5 are listed below:

First, the two sections in the aorta are split, making the 3D network more difficult to draw connections between the masks of the two sections. Second, the grayscale values of the two sections are significantly different because of the different speeds of blood flow in them, this feature confuses the network and makes it more difficult to recognize the correct grayscale of the aorta. Third, only 5 out of 56 samples have aortic dissection; the small amount of these pathological samples limits the information the network can learn.

4.2   Results on Validation Set 2

The performances of RASNet and U-Net-CSAM [5] are listed in Table 4, and the visualized 3D models of the segmentation results are shown in Fig. 8. Comparing the results of the two methods, our segmentation results include fewer false positives and false negatives than that given by U-Net-CSAM. RASNet is more accurate in segmenting the validation set, and the CBAM in all layers works better than the CSAM used as the bottom block between downward and upward sampling modules.

Table 4. Performances of our method and another method.

Method	Network	Image	D1	D3	K1	K3	R1	R3
RASNet	3D U-Net + CBAM	DSC	0.922	0.753	0.815	0.863	0.899	0.943
		HD	6.54	24.31	28.15	11.09	8.27	2.61
U-Net-CSAM	U-Net 176 + CSAM	DSC	0.877	0.318	0.585	0.779	0.803	0.749
		HD	9.48	33.35	12.48	6.97	5.12	19.04

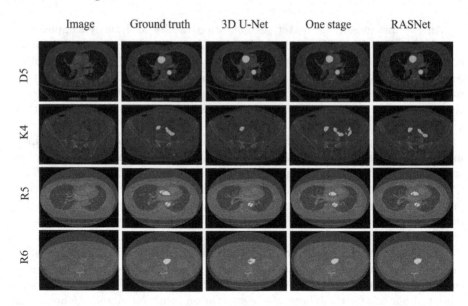

Fig. 5. Slices of segmentation results of different methods. From the first row to the last are the samples D5, K4, R5, R6. "One stage" means one-stage-trained network here.

4.3 Results on Test Set

The results on the 5 samples in the test set provided in the phase 2 of SEG.A are shown in Table 5. The average DSC is 0.8766 and the average HD is 20.6. In sample 3, the HD is significantly larger than the other samples', and the largest HD is 10 times larger compared to the smallest one. Basically the results on the test set are consistent with those on the validation set.

Table 5. Performances on test result of phase 2.

Case	0	1	2	3	4
Dice	0.918	0.892	0.835	0.864	0.874
HD	4.23	6.0	14.87	55.37	22.64

4.4 Limitation and Future Work

According to the segmentation results of the validation set and test set, our method's limitation is the instability of the HD, and the segmentation results on samples with aortic dissection need to be more accurate. Our future work will focus on reducing the maximum HD by testing different loss functions that are based on HD. Another potential method for improvement is the semi-supervised training with many unlabeled samples.

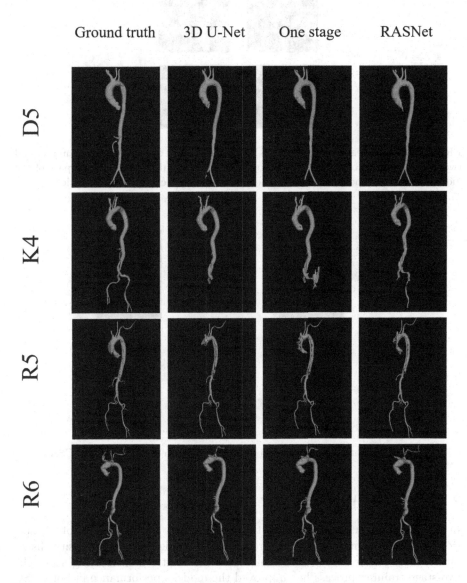

Fig. 6. Reconstruction models of segmentation results by different methods. From the first row to the last are the samples D5, K4, R5, R6.

108   J. Zhang et al.

Two stages (RASNet)   One stage

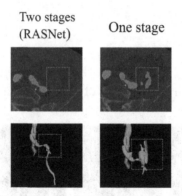

Fig. 7. Details of segmentation results of sample K4 by one-stage-trained model and two-stage-trained model. The one-stage-trained model mistakenly labeled part of the kidney as the false positive, which is demarcated with rectangular boundaries.

Ground truth   U-Net-CSAM   RASNet

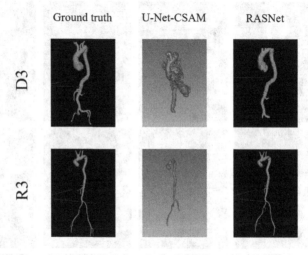

Fig. 8. Segmentation results on R3 and D3 by our method and U-Net-CSAM.

5 Conclusion

In the research on multicenter aorta segmentation, we propose a robust aortic segmentation method that decreases the heterogeneity of intensity distribution inter-center samples and fully uses the multicenter training sets. The two-stage training process has improved the model's performance in both DSC and HD. The 3D U-Net network with CBAM produces more attention on prominent regions than the baseline. The experiment results indicate the feasibility of automatic aortic segmentation in clinical practice.

Acknowledgement. This work was supported by the National Undergraduate Training Program for Innovation and Entrepreneurship (Grant NO. 202310386013) and the National Natural Science Foundation of China (62271149), Fujian Provincial Natural Science Foundation project (2021J02019).

References

1. Radl, L., Jin, Y., Pepe, A., et al.: AVT: multicenter aortic vessel tree CTA dataset collection with ground truth segmentation masks. Data Brief. **40**, 107801 (2022)
2. Jin, Y., et al.: AI-based aortic vessel tree segmentation for cardiovascular diseases treatment: status quo. arXiv preprint arXiv:2108.02998 (2021)
3. Deng, X., et al.: Graph cut based automatic aorta segmentation with an adaptive smoothness constraint in 3D abdominal CT images. Neurocomputing **310**, 46–58 (2018)
4. Cheung, W.K., Bell, R., Nair, A., et al.: A computationally efficient approach to segmentation of the aorta and coronary arteries using deep learning. IEEE Access **9**, 108873–108888 (2021)
5. Scharinger, B., Pepe, A., Jin, Y., et al.: Multicenter aortic vessel tree extraction using deep learning. In: Medical Imaging 2023: Biomedical Applications in Molecular, Structural, and Functional Imaging. SPIE, vol. 12468, pp. 341–347 (2023)
6. Sato, J., Kido, S.: Large batch and patch size training for medical image segmentation. arXiv preprint arXiv:2210.13364 (2022)
7. Karimi, D., Salcudean, S.E.: Reducing the Hausdorff distance in medical image segmentation with convolutional neural networks. IEEE Trans. Med. Imaging **39**(2), 499–513 (2019)
8. Woo, S., Park, J., Lee, J.-Y., Kweon, I.S.: CBAM: convolutional block attention module. In: Ferrari, V., Hebert, M., Sminchisescu, C., Weiss, Y. (eds.) ECCV 2018. LNCS, vol. 11211, pp. 3–19. Springer, Cham (2018). https://doi.org/10.1007/978-3-030-01234-2_1
9. Milletari, F., Navab, N., Ahmadi, S.A.: V-Net: fully convolutional neural networks for volumetric medical image segmentation. In: 2016 Fourth International Conference on 3D Vision (3DV), pp. 565–571. IEEE (2016)
10. Pepe, A., et al.: Detection, segmentation, simulation and visualization of aortic dissections: a review. Med. Image Anal. **65**, 101773 (2020). https://doi.org/10.1016/j.media.2020.101773
11. Heller, N., et al.: The KiTS19 challenge data: 300 kidney tumor cases with clinical context, CT semantic segmentations, and surgical outcomes. arXiv preprint arXiv:1904.00445 (2019)
12. Zhao, B., et al.: Data From RIDER_Lung CT. The Cancer Imaging Archive (2015). https://doi.org/10.7937/K9/TCIA.2015.U1X8A5NR

Optimizing Aortic Segmentation with an Innovative Quality Assessment: The Role of Global Sensitivity Analysis

Gian Marco Melito[1]([✉])(iD), Antonio Pepe[2](iD), Alireza Jafarinia[3](iD), Thomas Krispel[4](iD), and Jan Egger[2,5](iD)

[1] Graz University of Technology, Institute of Mechanics, Kopernikusgasse 24/IV, 8010 Graz, Austria
gmelito@tugraz.at
[2] Graz University of Technology, Institute of Computer Graphics and Vision, Inffeldgasse 16/II, 8010 Graz, Austria
[3] Graz University of Technology, Institute of Strength of Materials, Kopernikusgasse 24/I, 8010 Graz, Austria
[4] Graz University of Technology, Institute of Fundamentals and Theory in Electrical Engineering, Inffeldgasse 18, 8010 Graz, Austria
[5] University Hospital Essen, Institute for Artificial Intelligence in Medicine, Girardetstraße 2, 45131 Essen, Germany

Abstract. Precise aortic vessel tree segmentation is critical in the continuously evolving medical imaging domain. This study highlights the role of global sensitivity analysis in stimulating innovation in quality assessment techniques for aortic segmentation. In this methodology paper, we propose a novel method that integrates global sensitivity analysis with data augmentation techniques, aiming to enhance the reliability and robustness of segmentation algorithms. This approach aims to quantify the challenges posed by image variations and aspires to establish a methodology capable of managing a spectrum of image scenarios. The study also explores the implications of achieving accurate segmentations for clinical monitoring and computational fluid dynamics simulations of the aortic vessel tree. The presented approach was used for the final ranking of the MICCAI 2023 SEG.A. challenge to account for image variations in evaluating the submitted algorithms.

Keywords: Sensitivity analysis · Multicenter dataset · Aortic segmentation

1 Introduction

In recent years, image segmentation has rapidly expanded, finding numerous applications [7], particularly in the medical domain [6]. Its capacity to extract critical patterns and features from simple CT or MRI scans enables physicians to identify essential characteristics in both diseased and healthy patients [23].

The SEG.A. challenge, held in collaboration with the prestigious MICCAI 2023 conference, aimed at testing the capabilities of algorithms designed to automatically

A. Pepe et al. (Eds.): SEGA 2023, LNCS 14539, pp. 110–126, 2024.
https://doi.org/10.1007/978-3-031-53241-2_9

segment the aortic vessel tree (AVT) in a series of CT scans and generate mesh representations for visualization and simulation purposes (https://multicenteraorta.grand-challenge.org/). The challenge sought to develop solutions that can accurately and efficiently extract the AVT geometry from the scans, paving the way for better diagnosis and treatment of aortic conditions. The participants were provided with CT scans from various centers such as hospitals and clinics [26]. Each center utilized different devices and settings, resulting in image production variations. These variations can stem from a myriad of factors, including patient conditions, the effectiveness of the contrast fluid at the time of scanning, and varying levels of machine noise across different centers [23].

Segmentation algorithms used in medical imaging often encounter difficulties due to their development on relatively small datasets of CT scans. These scans typically originate from a single clinic or employ a consistent acquisition technique, resulting in limited variability. This constraint poses a significant issue as it may not adequately capture the wide range of variations and uncertainties present in real-world clinical settings. Image augmentation techniques and resampling methods are frequently employed to address this shortage and augment the dataset. These methods are, however, frequently inaccurate, offering only a qualitative and limited expansion of the dataset's diversity [5, 16, 41]. To develop segmentation algorithms that are robust to diverse sources of uncertainties, it is necessary to quantify these variations and uncertainties meticulously. This work proposes an innovative approach to create quantitative variation within CT scans. This strategy is also designed to uncover the strengths and weaknesses of existing segmentation algorithms, providing a comprehensive analysis to guide improvements. Moreover, to accurately quantify the identified weaknesses, global sensitivity analysis (GSA) is employed.

GSA is a valuable tool in this context as it can systematically identify and distinguish between influential and non-influential factors within the data. It offers insights into how each element contributes to the overall uncertainty and variability in the segmentation process. By employing GSA, a detailed examination of the segmentation algorithms is possible, leading to an improved understanding of the algorithm and its optimization.

To accurately evaluate the quality of the reconstructed volumes, i.e., its ability to represent all the essential morphological features, it is necessary to consider specific metrics, like the Dice Similarity Coefficient (DSC) and the Hausdorff Distance (HD) [15, 22, 35]. Once CT acquisition is completed, the algorithm seeks to reconstruct the volumetric geometry of the aorta. The quality of this reconstruction is typically assessed using these two metrics, considering their mean value and standard deviation. However, in medium- to large-size datasets, the mean value and standard deviation may not provide meaningful conclusions about the reconstruction quality, primarily when DSC and HD distributions are skewed. The reliance solely on mean value and standard deviation for quantifying HD and DSC proves insufficient, necessitating the incorporation of additional statistical measures like skewness, median, and mode for a more comprehensive evaluation.

Large datasets of CT scans often introduce significant variations in image quality originating from diverse sources. For instance, patients experiencing acute pain may assume positions unsuitable for optimal scanning procedures. Sudden movements from patients can similarly impact image quality. Moreover, the efficiency of contrast fluid injected during the process and different machine noise levels across various centers can further influence the final quality of the scans. In this article, we propose a method that considers all the aforementioned variations to better estimate the performance of a segmentation algorithm. One key feature of the proposed method is using GSA as a tool to understand and quantify the influence of parameters related to image variations on the performance of the segmentation algorithm.

GSA aims at analyzing the impact of the input variables on the model's output and, therefore, getting a better comprehension of the model mechanics [4,13,20]. It has guided researchers to create models that are both less complex and more accurate. In a study from Melito et al. [21], GSA was a key player in helping choose the right model assumptions and helped identify inaccuracies in blood flow simulation assumptions. The value of GSA in enhancing research quality is substantial, highlighting its usefulness as a means for researchers seeking to improve the accuracy and reliability of their computational models [27].

In order to conduct a successful GSA, a significant amount of data is required. However, clinical data is often insufficient, posing a challenge for conducting deeper analyses. To address this challenge, a solution has been proposed in Jafarinia et al. [13] that involves generating virtual patient data by taking into consideration the probability distributions of the physiological input variables. This approach has been shown to be effective in overcoming the issue of limited data availability. Likewise, in the current article, data augmentation techniques are used to generate a virtual patient database, allowing for GSA and enabling the assessment of the segmentation algorithm through quantitative measures. In detail, the original clinical dataset from the CT scans undergoes data augmentation techniques encompassing geometric transformations such as angle variation and image motion, intensity operations mimicking different contrast fluid absorption levels, and noise injection simulating varying image quality.

The ultimate goal of the MICCAI 2023 SEG.A. challenge was to develop a robust algorithm capable of handling a spectrum of image scenarios and variations. An often desirable feature of developed models is their additivity, i.e., the ability to deal with different variations separately, having little or no interaction. Therefore, it becomes vital to quantify the influence of image variations on the algorithm's results. Also, the goal of one subtask in the challenge was to create accurate and high-quality volume meshes. This aspect is indeed crucial for conducting computational fluid dynamics (CFD) simulations within the AVT.

Biomedical researchers have employed CFD to explore various aspects of cardiovascular health, including congenital heart disease, heart failure, ventricle function, aortic diseases, and cerebrovascular diseases [19]. CFD simulations offer distinctive insights into vascular health and disease management, making them valuable tools for both researchers and clinicians, for instance, in decision-making and personalized surgical planning [10]. With reduced hardware costs and faster computing simulations, CFD is becoming increasingly reliable for delivering precise results in health care. Many studies have used image-based CFD simulations to give a better understanding of diseases associated with AVT [1–3,12–14,24,30,36]. However, despite its immense

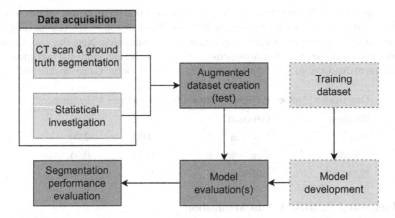

Fig. 1. Strategy schematics for segmentation quality assessment. After the initial data acquisition and the creation of the augmented test dataset, new model evaluations are performed. Successively, statistical analysis and GSA are performed on the resulting model outcomes and included in the segmentation performance evaluation block. Note that the augmented dataset is used as a test set for the developed segmentation model, while the training dataset is employed exclusively for the development of the model, neither of which is covered in this study.

potential, the adoption of CFD in the biomedical field has been slower due to the intricate nature of human anatomy and fluid behavior within the body. Accurate modeling of human anatomy and mesh generation is the first and most important step in enabling stable, accurate, and fast CFD simulation. The MICCAI 2023 SEG.A. challenge provided an initial attempt to generate robust mesh generation.

In this study, the collection of medical images and their respective ground truth segmentations are analyzed, including the study of image variations variables and their statistical distribution. Next, it is defined how augmented CT scans are developed along with their ground truth segmentations, and the algorithm used for this process. Subsequently, an introduction to GSA is provided, laying a foundation for a detailed exposition of the quality assessment metrics for segmentation algorithms.

2 Materials and Methods

In order to improve medical imaging segmentation, it is crucial to have a comprehensive approach accounting for potential uncertainty sources, especially when it comes to AVT segmentation. Our approach, detailed in the following sections and depicted in the schematics in Fig. 1, seeks to streamline and improve the quality assessment of the segmentation process, connecting statistical and analytical techniques. Initially, our method focuses on gathering imaging data and their potential variations. By creating augmented or virtual test datasets, the quality assessment of the algorithms is enriched by incorporating probabilistic factors. As the final step, we take a critical look at the performance of the segmentation algorithms, developing metrics that offer both a measure of their effectiveness and insights into potential areas for further improvement.

Table 1. Summary of the four principal image variation variables (rotation, motion, contrast, and noise standard deviation), their corresponding probability distribution functions (uniform or Gaussian), and the respective parameters governing each distribution. Note that two parameters are sufficient to characterize both distributions used in this study: minimum and maximum values for the uniform distribution, and mean and standard deviation for the Gaussian distribution.

Description	Name	Probability distribution	Parameter 1	Parameter 2
Rotation	α	Gaussian	0.00	5.00
Motion	d	Uniform	0.00	2.00
Contrast	β	Gaussian	0.00	0.05
Noise std	σ_n	Uniform	0.00	0.03

2.1   Image and Statistical Data Acquisition

First, the collection and organization of medical image data are performed. In particular, CT scans and ground-truth segmentations, carried out by specialized physicians, are collected and stored. We relied on the NRRD file format, which also ensures data anonymization as it does not store DICOM tags [17]. A public dataset of aortic vessel trees is provided by Radl et al. [26].

Successively, statistical variations for the image data are gathered. To complete this task, it is essential to conduct a thorough analysis of the existing literature and collect expert opinions and professional experiences. Throughout our study, however, we encountered a lack of specific data in the existing literature. As a result, we relied heavily on experience and knowledge and sought, therefore, expert advice to identify potential variations in certain variables. These variations were treated as potential sources of uncertainty. It is important to note, however, that assumptions on such sources require validation through more exhaustive studies in the future.

Different image augmentation techniques are employed in this study, resulting in 4 variables. The specifics of image augmentation variables are reported in Table 1 and visually represented in Fig. 2. Each variable follows a unique probability distribution function, essential for the sensitivity analysis study. Each probability distribution has been drawn to systematically simulate the source of uncertainty in the input data. The parameters that define their characteristics are obtained through the expertise of professionals in the field.

2.2   Augmented Dataset Creation

In recent advancements, data augmentation has emerged as a powerful technique to synthesize supplementary training data by applying fundamental transformations. This strategy addresses the downside of constrained or imbalanced datasets, which may lead to model overfitting and compromise model efficiency. Expanding the training dataset's size and heterogeneity via data augmentation increases the model's generalization capacity and enhances predictive outcomes [5, 8, 31]. While image augmentation is a frequently observed practice, it is notable that details regarding the statistical distribution of the variables during the augmentation process often remain undisclosed, leaving a gap in the comprehensive understanding of the study.

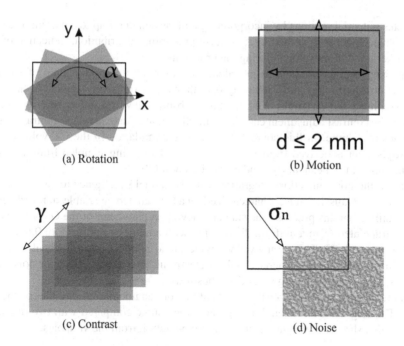

Fig. 2. Visual representation of the image variation variables employed in the augmentation process, i.e., (a) rotation, (b) motion, (c) contrast, and (d) noise. The original CT scan is depicted as an empty rectangle, with the applied augmentation operations highlighted in red. The black arrows indicate the scan reference system and the white arrows identify the corresponding applied image variation. (Color figure online)

In this study, the data augmentation technique serves as a tool to create a diverse dataset from the original one and is used as a test set for the segmentation algorithm. This facilitates the analytical investigation of the algorithm's sensitivity to variations in the input data. The proposed approach is essential in assessing the model's reliability and resilience across several scenarios, culminating in boosted accuracy and reliability in image reconstructions.

Geometric transformations are crucial in image processing, particularly in medical imaging. Specifically, rotation is a geometric transformation applied to CT volumes to modulate the orientation of the scan. Positioning the patient not perfectly supine on the CT table is sometimes unavoidable due to pathological complications of the patient. Although the available clinical software usually resamples such cases directly after image acquisition, this paper aims to quantify the resulting variations to optimize segmentation from raw data. Therefore, angle variations are simulated in the image augmentation process. In this study, rotations are imposed parallel to the z-axis (patient vertical axis), with the rotation angle α being extrapolated from a normal distribution characterized by a mean value of 0 degrees and a standard deviation of 5 degrees.

The simulation of patient motion represents a critical factor in medical image processing. During scanning, movements can induce blurring and introduce artifacts within the reconstructed volume, potentially leading to diagnostic inaccuracies. This study simulates potential motions by incorporating a displacement d up to a margin of 2 mm. This displacement is governed by a uniform probability distribution, indicative of the equal likelihood of movement during the procedure.

Intensity operations stand as prevalent techniques in the modification of medical image contrasts. In this study, intensity operations are exclusively applied to the AVT area to replicate the variations in contrast fluid absorption witnessed in patients. Consequently, the contrast adjustment can either amplify or attenuate the AVT contrast within the thoracic volume. In this context, the gamma formulation in the CT volume contrast adjustment is derived from $\gamma = e^\beta$, with β values being sampled from a normal distribution with 0 mean and a standard deviation of 0.05.

Lastly, the noise injection integration tests the model's resilience to varying image quality levels. Gaussian noise, characterized by a 0 mean and a variable standard deviation, is utilized in this process. The standard deviation parameter of the Gaussian noise σ_n is extrapolated from a uniform distribution with a range spanning from 0 to a maximum value of 0.03. This strategy finds widespread application in medical imaging, addressing potential noise sources such as electronic interference, detector noise, and artifacts, thereby contributing to model robustness.

In Fig. 3, we have illustrated the effects of the four augmentation variables on the CT scans. The original CT scan and its segmentation can be compared with two modified versions that showcase varying degrees of augmentation from the variables.

Implementation. In this study, we employed *TorchIO* [25], a Python library developed for 3D medical images, to construct the image augmentation algorithm. At the heart of our algorithm, as described in Fig. 4, there are three key inputs: the original CT scan, the ground truth segmentation, and a set of N_s image variation samples. These samples, delineated as rotation, motion, contrast, and noise, are formulated based on uniform or Gaussian probability distribution functions.

The algorithm operates by first selecting one sample (denoted with index n) from the variation set to separately augment the ground truth segmentation and the CT scan. Specifically, only a rotational adjustment is applied to the ground truth segmentation to create its augmented version. Simultaneously, the original ground truth segmentation facilitates the extraction of a mask, which is employed to identify the specific region within the original CT scan that will undergo the contrast adjustments. Once this step is completed, the algorithm integrates the remaining transformations (rotation, motion, and noise) onto the original CT scan, thereby yielding an augmented version of the scan, ready for the next phase of evaluation.

The outputs generated by the algorithm - the augmented ground truth segmentation and the adjusted CT scan - play a key role in evaluating the efficacy of a subsequent segmenting algorithm. Using the augmented CT scan as input for the segmentation algorithm, a new segmentation process is initiated, producing a new set of data. This freshly segmented data is then meticulously compared with the augmented ground truth segmentation to calculate the quality evaluation metrics: DSC and HD. These metrics serve as reliable indicators of the accuracy and effectiveness of the new segmenting algorithm, providing a comprehensive insight into the potential and precision of our image augmentation algorithm in real-world applications, e.g. CFD simulations.

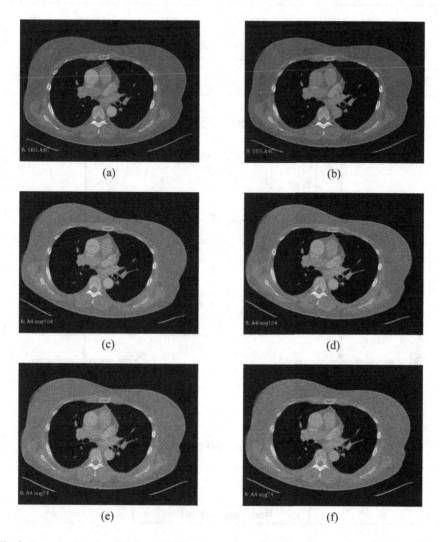

(a)   (b)

(c)   (d)

(e)   (f)

Fig. 3. Comparative visualization of original and augmented CT scans. (a) Original CT scan, (b) original CT scan with a red overlay indicating segmentation, (c) and (d) augmented CT scan variations with corresponding segmentations showcased, (e) and (f) further augmented CT scan examples demonstrating the diverse impacts of the applied variations on the segmentation, depicted in a green overlay. All the image augmentation variables are employed for the production of the augmented CT scans, i.e., rotation, motion, contrast, and noise. (Color figure online)

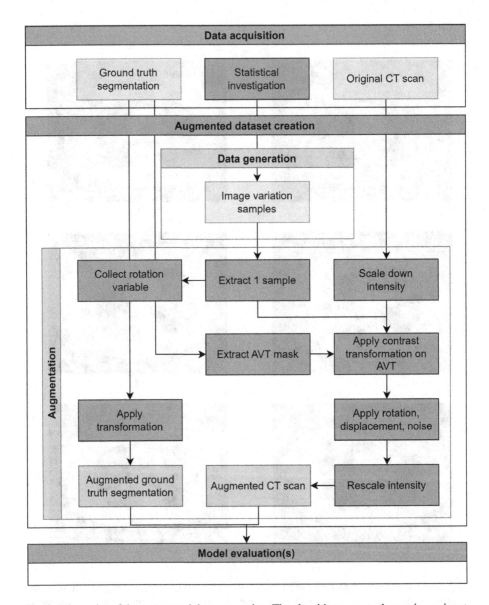

Fig. 4. Schematics of the augmented dataset creation. The algorithm accepts three primary inputs (in yellow): an original CT scan, its ground truth segmentation, and the image variation samples generated from a statistical investigation. The variations include rotation, motion, noise, and contrast. Within the algorithm, individual samples are employed to augment the CT scan and the ground truth segmentation separately, culminating in the generation of two refined outputs (in red): the augmented CT scan and the augmented ground truth segmentation. (Color figure online)

2.3   Global Sensitivity Analysis

In evaluating the effect of input variables on the outcome quantities of interest within a system, a GSA serves as an indispensable tool. Given the absence of preliminary insights into the individual or combined influences of the parameters on the output, we adopt a variance-based method employing the Sobol' indices [32,33]. For a given model f characterized by a multivariate random variable or vector, $x = [x_1, \ldots, x_i, \ldots, x_M]$ which belongs to $\mathbb{R}^M$, where M represents the number of input variables in the model, and a scalar output $Y = f(x)$ that lies in $\mathbb{R}$, the first and the total Sobol' indices are given as

$$S_i = \frac{\mathbb{V}\left[\mathbb{E}\left[Y|x_i\right]\right]}{\mathbb{V}\left[Y\right]}, \tag{1}$$

and

$$S_i^T = 1 - \frac{\mathbb{V}\left[\mathbb{E}\left[Y|x_{\sim i}\right]\right]}{\mathbb{V}\left[Y\right]} = \frac{\mathbb{E}\left[\mathbb{V}\left[Y|x_{\sim i}\right]\right]}{\mathbb{V}\left[Y\right]}. \tag{2}$$

Within these equations, the symbols $\mathbb{V}\left[\cdot\right]$ and $\mathbb{E}\left[\cdot\right]$ represent the statistical variance and expectation operators, respectively. The symbol $[\cdot|\cdot]$ represents the conditional operator, which conveys the variance or expectation of one variable in the context of another fixed variable. Notably, the conditional variance in Eq. 2, is computed over the whole input space except the i-th random variable and reported as $x_{\sim i}$.

The first Sobol' index, as in Eq. 1, is a useful tool for determining the individual impacts of different variables on the outcome of a model. Its value aids at defining a ranking of significance for all input variables based on their influence on the outcome. In contrast, the total Sobol' index considers the whole effect of the variables on the model, including the interactions between them. Therefore, it can identify factors that are not crucial for computational considerations and can be treated as model constants. By comparing the first and total Sobol' indices, it is possible to assess the extent of interaction occurring between input parameters [29].

The calculation of these indices can be performed using various techniques, including Monte Carlo sampling or quasi-Monte Carlo sequences [28,29]. However, to achieve the convergence on the indices values using these methods, a significant amount of model computations is necessary [11]. Thus, we opted for the implementation of a surrogate model, specifically the polynomial chaos expansion (PCE), to evaluate the indices from the coefficients derived from the expansion [9,18,34,37,39].

The standard random vector ξ is used to represent the vector x through an isoprobabilistic transformation, given the independent nature of input random variables x_i [34]

$$x = T(\xi), \quad \xi = \{\xi_1, \ldots, \xi_M\}. \tag{3}$$

Consequently, for the output Y having a finite variance, i.e., $\mathbb{V}\left[Y\right] < \infty$, the PCE $\widetilde{f}(x)$ is considered as a surrogate of the original model and is defined as

$$\widetilde{f}(x) = \sum_{\alpha \in \mathcal{A}} c_\alpha \Psi_\alpha(\xi), \tag{4}$$

where $\alpha = (\alpha_1, \ldots, \alpha_M)$ denotes a multi-index defined in $\mathcal{A} \subseteq \mathbb{Z}_0^M$, c_α represents the polynomial coefficients, and $\Psi_\alpha(\xi)$ are multivariate polynomials. The multivariate polynomials are derived for the standard random vector ξ as a function of univariate polynomials ψ_{α_i} as

$$\Psi_\alpha(\xi) = \prod_{i=1}^{M} \psi_{\alpha_i}(\xi_i). \tag{5}$$

Here, for a polynomial of degree p, $\alpha_i \geq 0$, and $\sum_{i=1}^{M} \alpha_i \leq p$. Moreover, the univariate polynomials $\psi_{\alpha_i}(\xi_i)$ adhere to orthogonality with respect to the i-th input probability distribution function. For the case of this study, Hermite polynomials are employed for Gaussian distributed variables, and Legendre polynomials for the uniformly distributed [9, 37, 38, 40].

The PCE is generally employed not only as a surrogate model but also for accurately calculating the Sobol' indices and performing sensitivity analysis [18, 34]. When employing PCE, the Sobol' indices can be directly calculated from the coefficients of the expansion c_α, proving to be more computationally efficient compared to conventional methods like Monte Carlo sampling. Given two additional sets of indices, namely

$$\mathcal{A}_i = \{\alpha \mid \alpha_i > 0 \wedge \alpha_j = 0 \quad \forall j \neq i\}, \tag{6}$$

and

$$\mathcal{A}_{T,i} = \{\alpha \mid \alpha_i > 0\}, \tag{7}$$

the first Sobol' index can be computed as

$$S_i = \frac{\sum_{\mathcal{A}_i} c_\alpha^2}{\sum_{\mathcal{A}} c_\alpha^2}. \tag{8}$$

Similarly, the total-order Sobol' index is computed as

$$S_i^{\mathrm{T}} = \frac{\sum_{\mathcal{A}_{T,i}} c_\alpha^2}{\sum_{\mathcal{A}} c_\alpha^2}. \tag{9}$$

The resulting sensitivity indices, computed using the PCE coefficients, allow for a detailed examination of the influence and interaction of input variables on the model output [18, 34]. Additionally, the surrogate model is a fast and accessible tool for computing model outputs, unlike the computationally expensive segmentation algorithm.

2.4   Quality Assessment Metrics

As the last step in the optimization workflow, a total of Ns augmented CT scan data are gathered, along with their corresponding segmentations that were generated in the augmented dataset creation step. In order to evaluate the accuracy of the segmentation algorithm, a comparison between the segmented images and the augmented ground truth data is conducted. This results in a comprehensive set of outputs that includes

DSC_n and HD_n values, for $n = 1, \ldots, N_s$. The quality evaluation of the segmentation algorithm is based on 4 new metrics formulated in this section.

Along with using DSC and HD to evaluate the segmentation algorithm, we introduce the application of Sobol' sensitivity indices. These indices are employed to assess the impact of the image variations described before on the designated evaluation metrics (DSC, HD). The Sobol' indices assist in identifying the extent of influence of each individual input variable, as well as their joint interactions, exert on the metrics. Since the aim of this study is to facilitate the development of a segmentation algorithm that demonstrates robustness against diverse image variations, a set of criteria has been devised. The variables in this study are considered independent and not correlated.

The metrics of evaluation, DSC and HD, should be proportionately affected by each image variation to guarantee the robustness of the algorithm across all variations uniformly. A model that distributes the influence of each input variable equally enhances balance and resilience within the system. This uniform distribution guarantees that the model is not excessively dependent on changes in a single input variable. Also, this approach simplifies the model optimization process since it allows uniform variable adjustment and management with the understanding that they have a consistent impact on the outcome. The uniform impact of image variations on the segmentation algorithm is monitored through the first Sobol' indices. The introduced metric $p_{1,k}$ is given as

$$p_{1,k} = 1 - \sum_{i=1}^{M} |S_{i,k} - 1/M| , \qquad (10)$$

where k indicates whether $p_{1,k}$ refers to the DSC or HD metric. A value of $p_{1,k}$ near the unity indicates a desirable uniform distribution of the first Sobol' indices, which corresponds to the ideal scenario.

Furthermore, it is essential that the segmentation algorithm ensures minimal interaction between different image variations. This characteristic ensures that the segmentation algorithm is able to cope with each image variation singularly, leading to an additive-like model. An additive model is defined when the outcome is expressed as a cumulative sum of independent variables, and where each variable affects the outcome independently without being affected by other variables. Among the benefits of an additive model, there is better predictive accuracy due to reduced noise and variability in predictions, simpler model adjustment in case of new implementation, and easier validation and understanding of the model's mechanics. To ensure this, parameter $p_{2,k}$ is evaluated by comparing the disparity between the total and first Sobol' indices, expressed as

$$p_{2,k} = \sum_{i=1}^{M} \left(S_{i,k}^{T} - S_{i,k} \right) . \qquad (11)$$

Optimally, p_2 should approximate zero, indicative of absent interactions between the variables. A visual representation of imperfect and ideal Sobol' indices distribution is given in Fig. 5.

As for the HD evaluation metric, it is preferable to reach a narrow variation with a value gravitating towards zero, as illustrated in Fig. 6. Given a possible asymmetric

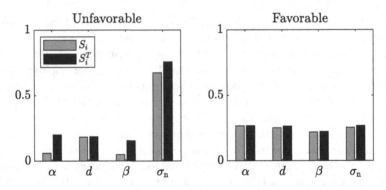

Fig. 5. Illustrative examples of favorable and unfavorable first and total Sobol' indices across image variation variables: rotation, motion, contrast, and noise standard deviation.

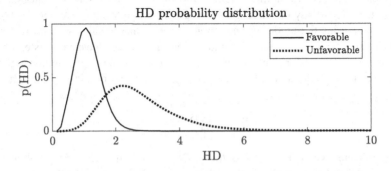

Fig. 6. Comparison of two probability distribution functions for the HD metric. The favorable distribution shows a reduced median, diminished variance, and more pronounced skewness relative to the unfavorable distribution.

distribution of the calculated HD, we incorporate the median (m_{HD}), variance (σ^2_{HD}), and skewness coefficient (μ_{HD}) for the evaluation of a new metric p_3(HD). Here, μ_{HD} is the Fisher's moment coefficient of skewness of the HD distribution, computed on the mean and variance of the distribution. Rather than the usual mean value, which suggests a symmetric distribution of the HD values (zero skewness and equal values of mean, median, and mode), our third proposed evaluation metric aims to consider a wider range of factors that impact HD performance. Finally, we introduce a ranking methodology for each distribution parameter to assess central tendency, spread, and asymmetry. To formulate the final metric p_3, we assign weights of 0.6, 0.25, and 0.15 to the median, variance, and skewness rankings, respectively, as

$$p_3 = 0.6r_{m_{HD}} + 0.3r_{\sigma^2_{HD}} + 0.15r_{\mu_{HD}}. \tag{12}$$

Conversely, the DSC evaluation metric is desired to exhibit a minimal variation, but with values leaning towards 1; see Fig. 7. The evaluation method for the fourth metric p_4(DSC) follows a similar approach to the p_3(HD) metric, including the assessments of the median (m_{DSC}), variance (σ^2_{DSC}), and skewness coefficient (μ_{DSC}) of the distribution,

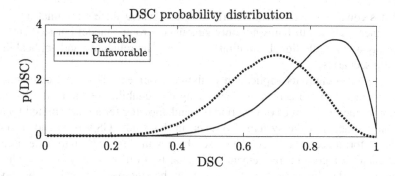

Fig. 7. Comparison of two probability distribution functions for the DSC metric. The favorable distribution shows a higher median, diminished variance, and lower skewness relative to the unfavorable distribution.

which are then ranked accordingly. These ranks are integrated with weights amounting to 0.6, 0.25, and 0.15, yielding to the final metric p_4, as

$$p_4 = 0.6 r_{m_{\mathrm{DSC}}} + 0.3 r_{\sigma^2_{\mathrm{DSC}}} + 0.15 r_{\mu_{\mathrm{DSC}}} . \tag{13}$$

Finally, for each criterion p_i, $i = 1, \ldots, 4$, we produce a ranking to assess the performance of the segmentation algorithm in each qualitative assessment. In the case of multiple algorithms, such as for model selection, a final computed ranking $r_{f,a}$ is obtained for each model a by taking a weighted average.

$$r_{f,a} = (r_{1,a} + r_{2,a})/6 + (r_{3,a} + r_{4,a})/3 . \tag{14}$$

The weights in Eqs. 12, 13, and 14 are computed to emphasize the importance of certain measures over others. They have been calibrated based on the desired outcome of the quality assessment.

3 Discussion and Conclusion

In this paper, we developed an innovative workflow for a thorough quality assessment of a segmentation algorithm that considers more detailed statistical information. Rather than employing the common mean value and standard deviation of DSC and HD, we employed the use of more comprehensive statistical parameters such as median, variance, and skewness to account for different statistical distributions. In addition to this, we introduced the use of sensitivity analysis to better identify the quality of the model in dealing with different sources of uncertainty. In this study, we employed rotation, motion, contrast, and noise augmentation variables to produce an enlarged test dataset for statistical and sensitivity analysis.

In the medical field, there is an increasing demand for a model that can maintain its robustness even when faced with various input variations. It is essential to have a reliable and consistent model that can provide accurate and trustworthy results, regardless of the changes in input. It is essential to develop a model such that each input variable contributes equally to the outcome variations, and where there's minimal interaction between them. These attributes not only guarantee a robust model but also ensure its adaptability against additional variations, enhancing its reliability and applicability in real-world scenarios.

Usually, GSA finds its application in the development phase of a computational model, aiding in the refinement and enhancing the reliability of the model by identifying non-influential sources of uncertainties and allowing for a concentrated focus on influential variables of the system. However, in this study, GSA is extended to evaluate the performance of a model. The use of GSA in this study marks the initiation of segmentation algorithm refinement. GSA can be further employed to reach other goals in model development. For instance, it can be employed to analyze the model's responsiveness to diverse image variations and to identify areas where the model may be lacking sensitivity. Furthermore, it can prove to be an essential tool in model reduction by evaluating the first and total Sobol' indices since noninfluential variables can be identified and prioritized based on their impact on the model.

We recognize the need for a more thorough examination of the image variation distributions as a limitation of this study. While the assumptions taken in this article are embedded in expert insights and experience, they require further investigation and validation. This realization opens new perspectives in research, urging a deeper analysis of medical image variations, which can further improve the existing methodology.

Acknowledgements. This work is supported by Graz University of Technology through the LEAD Project "Mechanics, Modeling, and Simulation of Aortic Dissection" and by the GCCE: Graz Center of Computational Engineering.

References

1. Armour, C.H., et al.: The influence of inlet velocity profile on predicted flow in type b aortic dissection. Biomech. Model. Mechanobiol. **20**, 481–490 (2021). https://doi.org/10.1007/s10237-020-01395-4

2. Armour, C.H., Menichini, C., Milinis, K., Gibbs, R.G.J., Xu, X.Y.: Location of reentry tears affects false lumen thrombosis in aortic dissection following tevar. J. Endovasc. Ther. **27**, 396–404 (2020). https://doi.org/10.1177/1526602820917962

3. Armour, Chlöe H., Menichini, C., Hanna, L., Gibbs, R.G.J., Xu, X.Y.: Computational modeling of flow and thrombus formation in type b aortic dissection: the influence of false lumen perfused side branches. In: Sommer, G., Li, K., Haspinger, D.C., Ogden, R.W. (eds.) Solid (Bio)mechanics: Challenges of the Next Decade: A Book Dedicated to Professor Gerhard A. Holzapfel, pp. 53–72. Springer International Publishing, Cham (2022). https://doi.org/10.1007/978-3-030-92339-6_2

4. Badeli, V., Melito, G.M., Reinbacher-Köstinger, A., Bíró, O., Ellermann, K.: Electrode positioning to investigate the changes of the thoracic bioimpedance caused by aortic dissection - a simulation study. J. Electr. Bioimpedance **11**, 38–48 (2020). https://doi.org/10.2478/joeb-2020-0007

5. Chlap, P., Min, H., Vandenberg, N., Dowling, J., Holloway, L., Haworth, A.: A review of medical image data augmentation techniques for deep learning applications. J. Med. Imaging Radiat. Oncol. **65**, 545–563 (2021). https://doi.org/10.1111/1754-9485.13261

6. Egger, J., et al.: Medical deep learning-a systematic meta-review. Comput. Methods Programs Biomed. **221**, 106874106874 (2022). https://doi.org/10.1016/j.cmpb.2022.106874

7. Egger, J., et al.: Deep learning-a first meta-survey of selected reviews across scientific disciplines, their commonalities, challenges and research impact. PeerJ Comput. Sci. **7**, e773 (2021). https://doi.org/10.7717/peerj-cs.773

8. Garcea, F., Serra, A., Lamberti, F., Morra, L.: Data augmentation for medical imaging: a systematic literature review. Comput. Biol. Med. **152**, 106391 (2023). https://doi.org/10.1016/j.compbiomed.2022.106391

9. Ghanem, R.G., Spanos, P.D.: Stochastic finite elements: a spectral approach. Springer, New York, NY (1991). https://doi.org/10.1007/978-1-4612-3094-6

10. Haggerty, C.M., et al.: Comparing pre- and post-operative fontan hemodynamic simulations: implications for the reliability of surgical planning. Ann. Biomed. Eng. **40**, 2639–2651 (2012). https://doi.org/10.1007/s10439-012-0614-4

11. Iooss, B., Lemaître, P.: A review on global sensitivity analysis methods. In: Uncertainty Management in Simulation-Optimization of Complex Systems, pp. 101–122. Springer, US (2015). https://doi.org/10.1007/978-1-4899-7547-8_5

12. Jafarinia, A., Armour, C.H., Gibbs, R.G.J., Xu, X.Y., Hochrainer, T.: Shear-driven modelling of thrombus formation in type b aortic dissection. Front. Bioeng. Biotechnol. **10**, 1033450 (2022). https://doi.org/10.3389/fbioe.2022.1033450

13. Jafarinia, A., et al.: Morphological parameters affecting false lumen thrombosis following type b aortic dissection: a systematic study based on simulations of idealized models. Biomech. Model. Mechanobiol. **22**, 885–904 (2023). https://doi.org/10.1007/S10237-023-01687-5

14. Jafarinia, A., Müller, T.S., Windberger, U., Brenn, G., Hochrainer, T.: Blood rheology influence on false lumen thrombosis in type b aortic dissection. J. Biomed. Eng. Biosci. **7**, 13–24 (2020). https://doi.org/10.11159/jbeb.2020.002

15. Jin, Y., et al.: AI-based aortic vessel tree segmentation for cardiovascular diseases treatment: Status quo (2021)

16. Kalidindi, A., Kompalli, P., Bandi, S., Anugu, S.: CT image classification of human brain using deep learning. Int. J. Online Biomed. Eng. **17**, 51 (2021)

17. Kodym, O., et al.: Skullbreak/skullfix-dataset for automatic cranial implant design and a benchmark for volumetric shape learning tasks. Data Brief **35**, 106902 (2021). https://doi.org/10.1016/j.dib.2021.106902

18. Le Gratiet, L., Marelli, S., Sudret, B.: Metamodel-based sensitivity analysis: polynomial chaos expansions and gaussian processes. In: Ghanem, R., Higdon, D., Owhadi, H. (eds.) Handbook of Uncertainty Quantification, pp. 1289–1325. Springer, Cham (2017). https://doi.org/10.1007/978-3-319-12385-1_38

19. Lee, B.K.: Computational fluid dynamics in cardiovascular disease. Korean Circ. J. **41**, 423 (2011). https://doi.org/10.4070/kcj.2011.41.8.423

20. Melito, G.M., Jafarinia, A., Hochrainer, T., Ellermann, K.: Sensitivity analysis of a phenomenological thrombosis model and growth rate characterisation. J. Biomed. Eng. Biosci. **7**, 31–40 (2021). https://doi.org/10.11159/jbeb.2020.004

21. Melito, G.M., Müller, T.S., Badeli, V., Ellermann, K., Brenn, G., Reinbacher-Köstinger, A.: Sensitivity analysis study on the effect of the fluid mechanics assumptions for the computation of electrical conductivity of flowing human blood. Reliab. Eng. Syst. Saf. **213**, 107663 (2021). https://doi.org/10.1016/j.ress.2021.107663

22. Müller, D., Soto-Rey, I., Kramer, F.: Towards a guideline for evaluation metrics in medical image segmentation. BMC. Res. Notes **15**(1), 1–8 (2022). https://doi.org/10.1186/s13104-022-06096-y

23. Pepe, A., et al.: Detection, segmentation, simulation and visualization of aortic dissections: a review. Med. Image Anal. **65**, 101773 (2020). https://doi.org/10.1016/j.media.2020.101773

24. Pirola, S., et al.: On the choice of outlet boundary conditions for patient-specific analysis of aortic flow using computational fluid dynamics. J. Biomech. **60**, 15–21 (2017). https://doi.org/10.1016/j.jbiomech.2017.06.005

25. Pérez-García, F., Sparks, R., Ourselin, S.: Torchio: a python library for efficient loading, preprocessing, augmentation and patch-based sampling of medical images in deep learning. Comput. Methods Programs Biomed. **208**, 106236 (2021). https://doi.org/10.1016/J.CMPB.2021.106236

26. Radl, L., et al.: AVT: multicenter aortic vessel tree CTA dataset collection with ground truth segmentation masks. Data Brief **40**, 107801 (2022). https://doi.org/10.1016/j.dib.2022.107801

27. Razavi, S., et al.: The future of sensitivity analysis: an essential discipline for systems modeling and policy support. Environ. Model. Software **137**, 104954 (2021). https://doi.org/10.1016/j.envsoft.2020.104954

28. Saltelli, A.: Making best use of model evaluations to compute sensitivity indices. Comput. Phys. Commun. **145**, 280–297 (2002). https://doi.org/10.1016/S0010-4655(02)00280-1

29. Saltelli, A., et al.: Global Sensitivity Analysis: The Primer. Wiley (2008). https://doi.org/10.1002/9780470725184

30. Schussnig, R., Dreymann, S., Jafarinia, A., Hochrainer, T., Fries, T.: A semi-implicit method for thrombus formation in haemodynamic fluid-structure interaction. In: CIMNE (2022). https://doi.org/10.23967/eccomas.2022.029

31. Shorten, C., Khoshgoftaar, T.M.: A survey on image data augmentation for deep learning. J. Big Data **6**, 60 (2019). https://doi.org/10.1186/s40537-019-0197-0

32. Sobol', I.M.: Global sensitivity indices for nonlinear mathematical models and their Monte Carlo estimates. Math. Comput. Simul. **55**(1–3), 271–280 (2001). https://doi.org/10.1016/S0378-4754(00)00270-6

33. Sobol', I.M.: On sensitivity estimation for nonlinear mathematical models. Matematicheskoe Modelirovanie **2**(1), 112–118 (1990)

34. Sudret, B.: Global sensitivity analysis using polynomial chaos expansions. Reliab. Eng. Syst. Saf. **93**(7), 964–979 (2008). https://doi.org/10.1016/j.ress.2007.04.002

35. Taha, A.A., Hanbury, A.: Metrics for evaluating 3D medical image segmentation: analysis, selection, and tool. BMC Med. Imaging **15**, 29 (2015). https://doi.org/10.1186/s12880-015-0068-x

36. Wang, K., Armour, C.H., Gibbs, R.G.J., Xu, X.Y.: A numerical study of the effect of thrombus breakdown on predicted thrombus formation and growth. Biomech. Model. Mechanobiol. 1–11 (2023). https://doi.org/10.1007/s10237-023-01757-8

37. Wiener, N.: The homogeneous chaos. Am. J. Math. **60**(4), 897 (1938). https://doi.org/10.2307/2371268

38. Xiu, D.: Numerical Methods for Stochastic Computations. Princeton University Press (2010). https://doi.org/10.1515/9781400835348

39. Xiu, D., Karniadakis, G.E.: Modeling uncertainty in steady state diffusion problems via generalized polynomial chaos. Comput. Methods Appl. Mech. Eng. **191**(43), 4927–4948 (2002). https://doi.org/10.1016/S0045-7825(02)00421-8

40. Xiu, D., Karniadakis, G.E.: The Wiener-Askey polynomial chaos for stochastic differential equations. SIAM J. Sci. Comput. **27**(3), 1118–1139 (2005). https://doi.org/10.1137/S1064827501387826

41. Zhang, L., et al.: Generalizing deep learning for medical image segmentation to unseen domains via deep stacked transformation. IEEE Trans. Med. Imaging **39**(7), 2531–2540 (2020). https://doi.org/10.1109/TMI.2020.2973595

A Mini Guide on Mesh Generation of Blood Vessels for CFD Applications

Domagoj Bošnjak$^{(\boxtimes)}$ and Thomas-Peter Fries

Institute of Structural Analysis, Graz University of Technology, Lessingstrasse 25,
Graz 8010, Austria
`bosnjak@tugraz.at`

Abstract. This work presents two topics relevant for mesh generation of blood vessels. Given a surface triangle mesh of the exterior part of a blood vessel, a short guide on meshing the inlets and outlets is provided. Namely, the open-source tool *Gmsh* is used to generate unstructured triangle and quadrilateral meshes, given a polyline description of a two-dimensional inlet or outlet. On the other hand, generating a three-dimensional mesh from the input surface mesh, suitable for fluid flow simulations, remains an open question. A small review of relevant methods for structured hexahedral meshing is provided, alongside arguments why they are in some cases preferred to the unstructured meshing approaches.

Keywords: Mesh generation · computational fluid dynamics

1 Introduction

The primary role of volumetric meshes of blood vessels is their use in numerical simulations, such as fluid flow or fluid-structure interaction simulations, e.g., based on the finite element method (FEM). Generally, approaches to the generation of such meshes can be split into *structured* and *unstructured* meshing approaches. Structured meshing is feasible when one can impose a structure on a domain, e.g., when working with simple geometrical shapes (cubes, cylinders, or similar) or variations of a single template-based domain. Otherwise, unstructured meshing is the only viable approach. The advantages of structured meshing include exact control of the number of elements and nodes, as well as the number of elements sharing a given node in the mesh. Furthermore, they can be tailored to the solution properties of the model equations, for example to account for singularities or boundary layers. A significant flaw of structured meshing is the lack of adaptability to an arbitrary domain, something available with the more robust, unstructured approaches. Clearly imposing structure on an arbitrary domain, in terms of topology and geometry, is certainly not a trivial task. Unstructured meshing is more flexible with respect to the features of the domain, bolstered by the availability of various commercial and open-source software [5,7,8,15]. However, the aforementioned properties of structured meshing are lost, such as the control over element and node number, and there is little control over the local element layout.

A. Pepe et al. (Eds.): SEGA 2023, LNCS 14539, pp. 127–134, 2024.
https://doi.org/10.1007/978-3-031-53241-2_10

Moreover, three-dimensional meshes can be categorized according to element types. Typical element types include tetrahedra and hexahedra, along with somewhat less utilized prisms and pyramids [17]. Thus, most meshes are either purely tetrahedral or hexahedral, though combinations of various elements are also possible. One such example are *hex-dominant* meshes, such as those presented in [12]. Typically, hexahedral meshes are more associated to structured meshing, and tetrahedral meshes to unstructured meshing, but it is not rigid, as, e.g., unstructured hexahedral meshing approaches exist as well [14].

In terms of computational fluid dynamics (CFD), a vital aspect that has to be considered already at the mesh level are *boundary layers*. During fluid flow through a blood vessel, typically no-slip conditions are imposed at the boundary, that is, the velocity exactly at the boundary is zero. However, the velocity then increases quickly when moving in normal direction of the boundary, leading to boundary layers near the walls. This often manifests through undesirable numerical properties, such as oscillations or convergence issues. Thus, one needs to take particular care of the mesh generation near the blood vessel walls. In this regard, element types can play a particularly important role. Resolution of boundary layers with hexahedra is undoubtedly more straightforward, as the common hex meshes of blood vessels are constructed in such a way that spatial refinement or mesh grading in the radial direction can be performed straightforwardly [3,6,16].

2   Unstructured Mesh Generation with Gmsh

For the purpose of this mini guide, we showcase directions to generate two-dimensional, unstructured, triangle meshes in *Gmsh* [5]. Such an approach may be applied to generate inlet and outlet meshes, given a surface mesh of the exterior of the domain, with an example in Fig. 1. From the triangle surface mesh of the exterior, we can directly extract contours of an inlet by intersecting the inlet plane with the surface mesh. This yields a two-dimensional polyline representation of a circle. Generally, the shape does not need to be circular for the remainder of the paper, but this structure is simply considered for simplicity reasons. To obtain proper matching with the exterior mesh, the surface of the two-dimensional inlet mesh must consist of exactly the points from the very same polyline. Figure 2 shows such a representation in Gmsh. In the case of a polyline input, i.e., a set of points and the segments connecting them, only two steps are necessary to generate an unstructured mesh. The first step includes creating a plane surface, based on the polyline boundary. Gmsh is capable of reading out the entire closed boundary automatically. From there on, a two-dimensional mesh can be generated. The two steps are shown in Fig. 3 and 4. Each point is associated with a mesh size parameter, which determines the local resolution of the mesh. Figure 6 showcases the same mesh with different local mesh size parameters. Moreover, several algorithms are available to recombine a triangle mesh into an unstructured quad mesh, such as the Blossom-quad [13]. An example of an unstructured quad mesh is shown in Fig. 7.

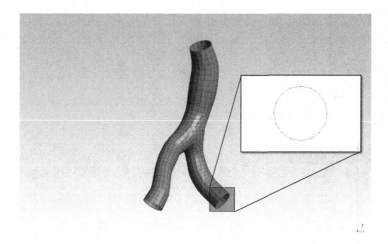

Fig. 1. An example of a quadrilateral surface mesh that only covers the exterior of a blood vessel, with circular outlets.

Fig. 2. The input polyline of a circle, also shown in Fig. 1.

3   Structured Mesh Generation for Blood Vessels

As mentioned, many unstructured mesh generators, such as Gmsh and tetgen, are able to produce a tetrahedral mesh from an input surface triangle mesh. Still, the process may not be as straightforward as obtaining a CFD-suitable mesh on the first try, i.e., additional user intervention is often necessary. On the other hand, generating structured, hexahedral meshes for cardiovascular domains comes with a set of potential advantages, though it remains an open topic, as developing a general algorithm which delivers a valid mesh for any input geometry presents a formidable challenge. We mention several relevant

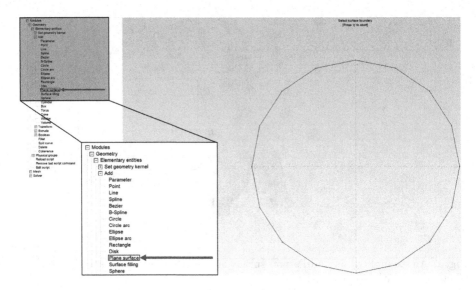

Fig. 3. Plane surface generation from a polyline.

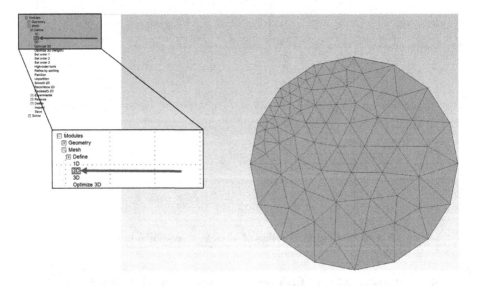

Fig. 4. Mesh generation from a polyline and a plane surface.

approaches. Blood vessels admit a natural centerline, also called a *(topological) skeleton* [2], which presents a natural foundation for structured meshing. As such, many approaches to this problem are skeleton-based, such as the adaptive hex meshing of general tubular shapes by Livesu et al. [9], and the patient-specific mesh generation approach based on a body-fitted coordinate system by Ghaffari et al. [6]. Skeletons may be used in conjunction with *scaffoldings*,

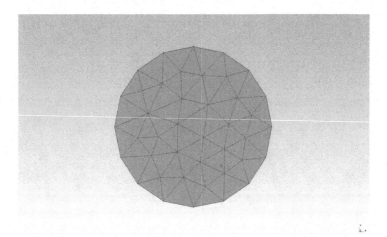

Fig. 5. An example of an unstructured triangle mesh, that conforms to the original boundary points.

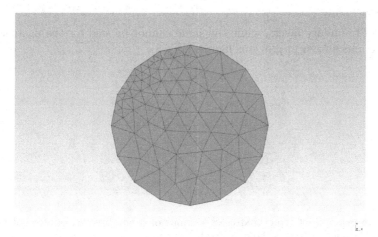

Fig. 6. The same mesh as the one in Fig. 5, with modified local mesh size at certain points.

namely coarse surface meshes of the domain of interest made of quadrilaterals [4, 10]. Moreover, there exist approaches based on *block-structures*, i.e., three-dimensional coarse-level approximations of the domain. Relevant works include the overview of CFD-suitable block-structured approaches given in [1], and a very recent skeleton-based block-structure approach from [3]. Additional recent contributions to this topic include the very extensive review of hexahedral meshing methods by Pietroni et al. [11], as well as an interactive hexahedral meshing tool presented in [18]. Finally, for comparison, we show the cross-sections from a seminal work on structured mesh generation of blood vessels, which enable

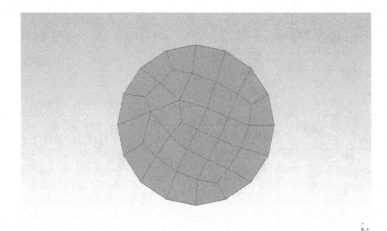

Fig. 7. An example of an unstructured quadrilateral mesh produced from the previously shown triangle mesh, by the Blossom recombination.

control of boundary layers, while the same cannot be said for the unstructured cross-sections shown in previous figures (Fig. 8).

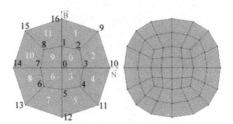

Fig. 8. An example of structured cross-sections of a blood vessel meshes taken from [16], offering good boundary layer control.

4 Conclusions

Generating CFD-suitable volumetric meshes from given surface meshes of blood vessels remains an open topic of research. Several approaches to this problem were discussed, mainly in terms of structured hexahedral meshing, backed by the usefulness of hexahedra in the resolution of boundary layers. Aside from that, we have presented a short guide related to unstructured meshing of inlets and outlets, given a surface mesh of the exterior of a blood vessel, performed in Gmsh.

Acknowledgements. The authors acknowledge the LEAD Project: Mechanics, Modeling and Simulation of Aortic Dissection.

References

1. Ali, Z., Dhanasekaran, P., Tucker, P., Watson, R., Shahpar, S.: Optimal multi-block mesh generation for CFD. Int. J. Comput. Fluid Dyn., 195–213 (2017). https://doi.org/10.1080/10618562.2017.1339351
2. Au, O., Tai, C., Chu, H., Cohen-Or, D., Lee, T.: Skeleton extraction by mesh contraction. ACM Trans. Graph. **27**(3), 1–10 (2008). https://doi.org/10.1145/1399504.1360643
3. Bošnjak, D., Pepe, A., Schussnig, R., Schmalstieg, D., Fries, T.: Higher-order block-structured hex meshing of tubular structures. Eng. Comput. (2023). https://doi.org/10.1007/s00366-023-01834-7
4. Fuentes Suárez, A., Hubert, E.: Scaffolding skeletons using spherical Voronoi diagrams: feasibility, regularity and symmetry. Comput.-Aided Des. **102**, 83–93 (2018). https://doi.org/10.1016/j.cad.2018.04.016. Proceeding of SPM 2018 Symposium
5. Geuzaine, C., Remacle, J.: GMSH: a 3-d finite element mesh generator with built-in pre- and post-processing facilities. IJNME **79**(11), 1309–1331 (2009). https://doi.org/10.1002/nme.2579
6. Ghaffari, M., Tangen, K., Alaraj, A., Du, X., Charbel, F., Linninger, A.: Large-scale subject-specific cerebral arterial tree modeling using automated parametric mesh generation for blood flow simulation. Comput. Biol. Med. **91** (2017). https://doi.org/10.1016/j.compbiomed.2017.10.028
7. Hahn, D.: Coronary artery centerline extraction in 3d slicer using VMTK based tools. Department of Medical Informatics, University of Heidelberg, p. 105 (2010)
8. Izzo, R., Steinman, D., Manini, S., Antiga, L.: The vascular modeling toolkit: a python library for the analysis of tubular structures in medical images. J. Open Source Softw. **3**(25), 745 (2018)
9. Livesu, M., Muntoni, A., Puppo, E., Scateni, R.: Skeleton-driven adaptive hexahedral meshing of tubular shapes. Comput. Graph. Forum **35**(7), 237–246 (2016). https://doi.org/10.1111/cgf.13021
10. Panotopoulou, A., Ross, E., Welker, K., Hubert, E., Morin, G.: Scaffolding a Skeleton, pp. 17–35, May 2018. https://doi.org/10.1007/978-3-319-77066-6_2
11. Pietroni, N., et al.: Hex-mesh generation and processing: a survey. ACM Trans. Graph. **42**(2) (2022). https://doi.org/10.1145/3554920
12. Ray, N., Sokolov, D., Reberol, M., Ledoux, F., Lévy, B.: Hex-dominant meshing: mind the gap! Comput.-Aided Des. **102**, 94–103 (2018). https://doi.org/10.1016/j.cad.2018.04.012
13. Remacle, J.F., Lambrechts, J., Seny, B., Marchandise, E., Johnen, A., Geuzainet, C.: Blossom-quad: a non-uniform quadrilateral mesh generator using a minimum-cost perfect-matching algorithm. IJNME **89**(9), 1102–1119 (2012). https://doi.org/10.1002/nme.3279
14. Sarrate, J., Ruiz-Gironés, E., Roca, X.: Unstructured and semi-structured hexahedral mesh generation methods. Comput. Technol. Rev. **10**, 35–64 (2014). https://doi.org/10.4203/ctr.10.2
15. Si, H.: TetGen, a delaunay-based quality tetrahedral mesh generator. ACM Trans. Math. Softw. **41**(2) (2015). https://doi.org/10.13140/RG.2.2.13915.85284/2

16. Vukicevic, A., et al.: Three-dimensional reconstruction and NURBS-based structured meshing of coronary arteries from the conventional x-ray angiography projection images. Sci. Rep. **8**, 1711 (2018). https://doi.org/10.1038/s41598-018-19440-9

17. Zienkiewicz, O., Taylor, R.: The Finite Element Method: The Basis, vol. 1. Butterworth-Heinemann, Oxford (2000)

18. Zoccheddu, F., Gobbetti, E., Livesu, M., Pietroni, N., Cherchi, G.: HexBox: interactive box modeling of hexahedral meshes. Comput. Graph. Forum **42**(5), e14899 (2023). https://doi.org/10.1111/cgf.14899

Aortic Segmentations and Their Possible Clinical Benefits

Christian Mayer[1]([✉]) [iD], Melanie Arnreiter[1], Barbara Karner[1], Sophie Hossain[1], Hannes Deutschmann[2], Daniel Zimpfer[1], and Heinrich Mächler[1]

[1] Division of Cardiac Surgery, Department of Surgery, Medical University of Graz,
Auenbruggerplatz 29, 8036 Graz, Austria
christian.mayer@medunigraz.at
[2] Division of Neuroradiology, Vascular and Interventional Radiology, Department of Radiology,
Medical University of Graz, Auenbruggerplatz 9, 8036 Graz, Austria

Abstract. Computed tomography angiography (CTA) studies of the thoracic and abdominal aorta are very common in the routine clinical practice. Aortic diseases often require individualized diagnostics and very specialized physicians performing elaborate procedures. The vessel also serves as a "transport highway" for catheter-based treatment options and implants in many different procedures. Segmentations of the aorta and its vascular tree might have the potential of enhancing clinical workflows and results. Manual segmentation is a very time-consuming process, therefore automated solutions are urgently needed.

Keywords: Cardiac Surgery · Vascular Surgery · Cardiology · Interventional Radiology · Computed Tomography Angiography · Aorta · Segmentations

1 Introduction

The aim of this paper is to provide technicians with basic information about aortic anatomy, aortic diseases, and treatment options. Furthermore, practical benefits of automated segmentations of the aorta and the vascular tree in the routine clinical setting are demonstrated.

1.1 Aortic Anatomy

The aorta is the main blood vessel carrying oxygen-rich blood from the heart to (vital) organs and literally every part of the body. The aorta first courses upwards from the heart, then after branching of the supraaortic vessels extends downwards through the diaphragm into the abdomen where it ends at the iliac bifurcation and splits into the two common iliac arteries. The Aorta can be divided into different anatomic parts [1].

Ascending Aorta. The ascending aorta begins at the orifice of the aortic valve which directs blood flow from the left ventricle of the heart to all vessels. The first few centimeters of the aorta are called the aortic root. The lumen has three small pockets there that are called the sinuses of Valsalva where the left and the right coronary arteries depart which supply the heart with blood. The aortic root ends with the sinotubular junction where the ascending aorta extends further upward where it continues as the aortic arch with the branching of the brachiocephalic trunk [1].

Aortic Arch. In the aortic arch the aorta changes its directions from running upward (cranially) to running downward (caudally) and it also traverses from the right side of the midline of the body to the left side. It gives rise to the three supraaortal vessels. From proximal to distal, there is the brachiocephalic trunk, which supplies the right arm and brain, the left common carotid artery, which supplies the left side of the brain and the left subclavian artery supplying the left arm [1].

Descending Aorta. The descending aorta runs down to the diaphragm after branching of the left subclavian artery. It gives rise to a variable number of smaller branches for example to the chest wall and the spinal cord [1].

Abdominal Aorta. The abdominal aorta begins after passing through the diaphragm through the aortic hiatus approximately at the level of the 12th thoracic vertebra. It gives rise to the visceral arteries. The first artery is the celiac trunk which supplies the liver, stomach, spleen, duodenum and pancreas. Afterwards there are the superior and inferior mesenteric arteries supplying mainly the small and large intestine. Between the two mesenteric arteries the left and right renal arteries are branching to the kidneys. The abdominal aorta finally bifurcates at the level of the 4th lumbar vertebra into the left and right common iliac arteries [2].

Common Iliac and Femoral Arteries. The common iliac and femoral arteries anatomically do not belong to the aorta, but they are very important structures for obtaining vascular access to the aorta for aortic and vascular procedures besides the radial artery. After a few centimeters the common iliac arteries give rise to the internal iliac arteries and continue as external iliac arteries further down to the lower limbs coursing anterior and inferior until they exit the pelvic girdle under the inguinal ligament where they are referred to as the femoral arteries. After some variable centimeters they give off the deep femoral arteries and continue further down. The section between this femoral bifurcation and the inguinal ligament usually is the preferred location for obtaining vascular access [2, 3].

1.2 Aortic Diseases

Aortic Aneurysm. An arterial vessel, such as the aorta, that is dilated for more than 1.5 times of its normal diameter is called aneurysmatic. Aortic aneurysms can occur in any part of the aorta and are often distinguished in abdominal or thoracic, albeit thoracoabdominal aneurysms exist as well. Aortic aneurysms pose a risk for spontaneous rupture that increases exponentially with size [4]. For example, for an aorta with a diameter of 5.0 cm the annual rupture risk is 1 percent, for 6.0 cm it is already 10 percent and for an aorta with more than 7 cm of diameter the annual risk is up to 50 percent. Untreated ruptures have nearly 100 percent mortality, but even with an emergency operation, mortality is estimated 30 percent or higher [4, 5].

Aortic Dissection and Acute Aortic Syndrome. Acute aortic dissection is a critical disease, in which the three wall layers of the aortic wall become separated in the medial layer through a primary intimal tear on the luminal side of the wall, separating the lumen into a true and false one. This dreadful disease has an untreated mortality of nearly 100 percent, besides being complex to be treated. Aortic dissections are classified into Stanford type A and type B dissections, depending if the pathology involves the part of the aorta before (type A) or after (type B) the left subclavian artery. This classification has numerous implications for clinical management of the disease and is also used for aneurysms.

Acute aortic dissection belongs to a group of diseases summarized under the term acute aortic syndrome. It is a group of diseases where patients present with characteristic "aortic pain" caused by potentially life-threatening aortic pathologies. The other diseases are penetrating aortic ulcer, intramural hematoma and traumatic transection, all having in common a defect in the aortic wall with risk of or impending rupture [4, 6].

Aortic Valve Stenosis. Aortic valve stenosis is the most common valvular disorder of the heart valves. While not directly an aortic disease, it is the heart valve separating and directing blood flow from the left ventricle of the heart to the aortic root. In aortic stenosis the opening of the valve orifice is impaired through calcified and degenerated valve leaflets, leading to increased pressure gradients and a reduction of the effective valve orifice area of less than one square centimeter. This leads to development of heart failure and an increased risk of sudden cardiac death. Untreated symptomatic aortic stenosis has an annual mortality of about 30 percent [7, 8].

1.3 Aortic Procedures

Aortic Surgery. Aortic surgery often involves resecting a diseased, for example aneurysmatic or dissected, segment of the aorta with a Dacron tube graft. Complexity of these procedures rises if multiple branches are affected and need to be re-implanted in the prosthesis like in the aortic arch. The frozen elephant trunk technique for example is a hybrid prosthesis for the aortic arch combining a stent-graft for the descending aorta on the distal side with a branched prosthesis for the arch vessels and ascending aorta on the proximal side [9]. For surgery of the thoracic aorta utilizing a cardiopulmonary by-pass pump is nearly always necessary, most of the time even circulatory arrest with selective antegrade cerebral perfusion [4, 10].

Aortic Interventions. In contrast to open surgical operations, the term "interventions" is often used to describe minimally invasive endovascular procedures in which the patient is not cut open. The fluoroscopically guided procedure is performed with special wires and catheters after attaining vascular access using a percutaneous puncture. Depending on the location and extent of the pathology, placing a stent-graft through vascular access in the groin is often possible. Stent-grafts are vascular prosthesis of Dacron attached to a metal framework. These stent-grafts can be collapsed to a small diameter of under one centimeter and then be released and expanded again at the desired region in the aorta or target vessel. This is made possible, as the metal frame of the stent-grafts are made of the metal nitinol, a nickel and titanium alloy, which exhibits a temperature dependent shape memory effect. Stentgrafts are collapsed in iced saline solution onto a delivery device which is inserted into the vessel and released gradually through the mechanism of the device reverting to its original size and shape under body temperature [11]. Insertion of stent-grafts is considered the treatment of choice for the descending aorta without bigger vascular branches. However, its application in anatomically more complex regions like the aortic root or the aortic arch is still very limited and technically demanding. Still, it may be possible with the use of customized stent-graft designs or fenestrated grafts [4, 12].

Other Endovascular Procedures. There are numerous vascular interventions where physicians have to navigate safely through the aortic vascular network. For example, aortic valve stenosis can either be treated with open surgery or with transcatheter valves called a "TAVI-procedure". In this procedure, the new aortic valve is collapsed on a catheter and is set free on the diseased native aortic valve after navigating through the aorta from the iliac vessels. Other vascular interventions include dilatation of stenosis of the renal or visceral arteries. Also, for neurovascular interventions it is often necessary to navigate through the aorta [8, 13, 14].

2 Manual Aortic Segmentation

Manual segmentation can be a time-consuming process, requiring highly specific knowledge about anatomic and radiologic properties of CTA scans, as well as proficiency with suitable software tools in creating the desired results.

The software tool that has been used for manual segmentation at our institution was the openly available program 3D Slicer Version 5.0.3 [15]. With this tool it is possible to convert DICOM files into the Nearly Raw Raster Data (NRRD) format, removing all patient specific data for further processing and sharing. The software tools provide semi-automatic functions to accelerate and simplify the segmentation process. One method is to interpolate manual segmentations between slices of the CTA scan. For this manual segmentation every five to ten slices with paint and erase has to be performed. In 3D slicer this can be further facilitated using the level tracing function. This function tries to draw a closed path within the same intensity range back to a starting point and therefore recognizes luminal borders automatically. This works better in areas with less artifacts which is often the case when processing "healthy" aortas, but not so often in pathologically CTAs like, e.g. in aortic dissections. When this step is completed, the slices can be interpolated. In 3D Slicer this function is called "fill between slices". One can then preview the result and make manual corrections in slices where the segmentation is not ideal and execute the function.

The segmentation time for yielding satisfactory results in healthy aortas are between thirty and ninety minutes for "healthy" aortas but can range up to six hours for pathologically CTA scans. This is due to intimal flaps and their movement artifacts, separate lumina, areas with decreased flow, intraluminal thrombi, entries and reentries and vascular kinking. Intimal flaps are vascular tissue separating true and false lumen that are created during the development of aortic dissections.

In general, the better the quality of the CTA scan (less artifacts and pathological findings), the better the segmentation process can be performed.

3   Possible Clinical Benefits of Automated Aortic Segmentations

Automated segmentations can abbreviate the time-consuming process of manual segmenting anatomic structures of interest. Despite their benefits, personal resources and time is scarce in the clinical routine, therefore an automated process can greatly decrease resources needed.

With the implementation of automatic segmentations clinicians can benefit in their everyday work by having additional information with one look of the diseased aorta at hand, enhancing their decision-making and therapeutic workflows. Additionally, it can aid in the assessment of complex pathologies as well as providing useful information for non-aortic interventions in "healthy" aortas. Segmentations can help visualizing complex and abstract findings to physicians and to their patients. They can reduce workloads of (aortic) ambulances and be implemented in risk evaluation processes.

Segmentations have the potential to facilitate interventional procedures, where stent-grafts and implants like valvular prostheses are sized according to CTA scans and the procedures are thereafter performed under fluoroscopy. They can improve results and ease the process of adapting implants and the procedure specifically to a certain patient which is crucial to planning and executing a certain procedure and prevent complications like endoleaks or stent-graft migration.

Segmentations can also easily be 3D printed. The printed models can be used for educational purposes as well as planning and sizing of implants for endovascular procedures or for simulation purpose.

4   Conclusion and Perspective

Today, there are numerous aortic as well as non-aortic procedures that would benefit immediately from having automated segmentations at hand. The first step is creating and validating an algorithm that works for "healthy" aortas and then extending this to pathological aortas, as seen in aortic dissection. This can facilitate the process of diagnosing, monitoring and managing these diseases.

Another area in which demand is high are endovascular interventions, where the sizing and customization part could be simplified with this technology. Additionally, these models can help in procedural planning and anticipating possible complications beforehand.

Another future perspective is the possibility of 3D printing vascular implants. Current implants are suboptimal in terms of their stiffness profile and elastomechanical behavior [16]. Having the ability of printing customized prostheses with higher aortophilic properties might not be so far away in the future.

In light of this, an interdisciplinary approach between specialized physicians, engineers, biomedical-, material- and computer scientists is needed to accomplish these goals.

Disclosure of Interests. The authors have no competing interests to declare that are relevant to the content of this article.

References

1. di Gioia, C.R.T., Ascione, A., Carletti, R., Giordano, C.: Thoracic aorta: anatomy and pathology. Diagnostics **13**, 2166 (2023)
2. Legg, J.S., Legg, L.M.: Abdominal aortic aneurysms. Radiol. Technol. **88**, 145–163 (2016)
3. Rajebi, H., Rajebi, M.R.: Optimizing common femoral artery access. Tech. Vasc. Interv. Radiol. **18**, 76–81 (2015)
4. Robinson, D., Mees, B., Verhagen, H., Chuen, J.: Aortic aneurysms: screening, surveillance and referral. Aust. Fam. Phys. **42**, 364–369 (2013)
5. Erbel, R., et al.: 2014 ESC Guidelines on the diagnosis and treatment of aortic diseases: Document covering acute and chronic aortic diseases of the thoracic and abdominal aorta of the adult. The task force for the diagnosis and treatment of aortic diseases of the European society of cardiology (ESC). Eur. Heart J. **35**, 2873–2926 (2014)
6. Ahmad, F., Cheshire, N., Hamady, M.: Acute aortic syndrome: pathology and therapeutic strategies. Postgrad. Med. J. **82**, 305–312 (2006)
7. Pujari, S.H., Agasthi, P.: Aortic Stenosis. StatPearls Publishing, St. Petersburg (2023)
8. Vahanian, A., et al.: 2021 ESC/EACTS guidelines for the management of valvular heart disease. Eur. Heart J. **43**, 561–632 (2022)
9. Di Marco, L., et al.: The frozen elephant trunk technique: European association for cardiothoracic surgery position and bologna experience. Korean J. Thorac. Cardiovasc. Surg. **50**, 1–7 (2017)
10. Sc, M., et al.: The American association for thoracic surgery expert consensus document: surgical treatment of acute type A aortic dissection. J. Thorac. Cardiovasc. Surg., 162 (2021)
11. Stoeckel, D., Pelton, A., Duerig, T.: Self-expanding nitinol stents: material and design considerations. Eur. Radiol. **14**, 292–301 (2004)
12. Aranson, N.J., Watkins, M.T.: Percutaneous interventions in aortic disease. Circulation **131**, 1291–1299 (2015)
13. Mayer, C., et al.: Transapical TAVI in chronic type A dissection. Eur. Surg. **54**, 170–172 (2022)
14. Clayton, B., Morgan-Hughes, G., Roobottom, C.: Transcatheter aortic valve insertion (TAVI): a review. British J. Radiol., 87 (2014)
15. Egger, J., et al.: GBM volumetry using the 3D slicer medical image computing platform. Sci. Rep., 3 (2013)
16. Agrafiotis, E., et al.: Global and local stiffening of ex vivo-perfused stented human thoracic aortas: a mock circulation study. Acta Biomater. **S1742–7061**(23), 00117–00124 (2023). https://doi.org/10.1016/j.actbio.2023.02.028

Author Index

Printed in the United States
by Baker & Taylor Publisher Services